A LECTURE

ON THE

SÁNKHYA PHILOSOPHY

A LECTURE

ON THE

SÁNKHYA PHILOSOPHY,

EMBRACING THE TEXT

OF THE

TATTWA SAMÁSA.

KAPILA,

JAMES ROBERT BALLANTYNE

GYAN

Published by

GYAN

Gyan Publishing House
5, Ansari Road
Daryaganj, New Delhi-110002
Phone: 011-47034999, 9811692060
E-mail: books@gyanbooks.com

Distribution Network
gyanbooks.com
India, USA, Canada, UK, Australia

ISBN: 978-93-6208-261-9 (HB)
First Published, 1850

2nd Impression 2024

Printed at: Gyan Press, Delhi.

A LECTURE ON THE SÁNKHYA PHILOSOPHY
Author: KAPILA, JAMES ROBERT BALLANTYNE

A LECTURE

ON THE

SANKHYA PHILOSOPHY.

A LECTURE

ON THE

SA'NKHYA PHILOSOPHY,

EMBRACING THE TEXT

OF THE

TATTWA SAMA'SA.

PRINTED FOR THE USE OF THE BENARES COLLEGE
BY ORDER OF GOVERNMENT N. W. P.

Mirzapore.

ORPHAN SCHOOL PRESS:—SUPT. R. C. MATHER.

1850.

PREFACE.

This Lecture, delivered in the session of 1849, is a sequel to those on the *Nyáya* Philosophy delivered to the senior class of pupils in the English Department of the Benares College, in 1848, "with the view of introducing them to the philosophical terminology current among their learned fellow-countrymen the pandits."

For selecting the *Tattwa-samása* as the text-book, there were two motives—the simplicity of its arrangement, and the extreme rarity of the work. Mr. Colebrooke (at p. 233. vol. 1st of his Essays) speaks of it as being uncertain whether the work were still extant; and few of the pandits appear to know it except by name.

J. R. B.

Benares College,
31*st July*, 1850.

SYNOPSIS OF THE CONTENTS.

A LECTURE

ON THE

SANKHYA PHILOSOPHY.

No. 1.—[The founder of the *Sánkhya* school of philosophy was *Kapila*. Two treatises are attributed to him—the *Sánkhya-pravachana* and the *Tatwa-samása*. The latter will form the text of the following observations. The commentary commences thus :—]

श्री गणेशाय नमः । श्री कपिलमुनये नमः । पञ्चविंशति तत्त्वेषु जन्मना ज्ञानमाप्तवान् । आदिसृष्टौ नमस्तस्मै कपिलाय महर्षये ॥

अथातस्तत्त्वसमासाख्यसांख्यसूत्राणि व्याख्यास्यामः ॥

No. 2.—Salutation to *Gaṇes'a!* Salutation to the great sage *Kapila!* Salutation to that great sage *Kapila* who, at the first creation, obtained, merely by birth, a knowledge of the twenty-five principles (*tatwa*).

Now we shall explain the aphorisms of the *Sánkhya*, which constitute what is called the Compendium of Principles.

[In saying that *Kapila* obtained his knowledge "merely by birth," the author means that *Kapila* differed from those other teachers who, after being born, received instruction before they were qualified to teach. *Kapila* is regarded as an incarnation of the deity.]

इह कश्चिद्ब्राह्मणस्त्रिविधेन दुःखेनाभिभूतः सांख्याचार्य्यं कपिलमहर्षिं शरणमुपागतः । स्वकुलनामगोत्रं स्वाध्यायार्थं निवेद्याह । भगवन् किमिह परं। किं याथातथ्यं । किं कृत्वा कृतकृत्यः स्यामिति । कपिल उवाच । कथयिष्यामि ।

No. 3.—A certain bráhman, aggrieved by the three kinds of pain, had recourse to the great sage *Kapila*, the teacher of the *Sánkhya*. Having declared his family, his name and race, and his desire of instruction, he said—"Holy Sir! What is of all things the most important? What is actual truth? And what must I do in order that I may have done what is fitting to be done?" *Kapila* replied—"I shall tell you."

[The Aphorisms of *Kapila* here follow.]

अष्टौ प्रकृतयः ।१। षोडश विकाराः ।२। पुरुषः ।३। त्रैगुण्यं ।४। संचरः ।५। प्रतिसंचरः ।६। अध्यात्मं ।७। अधिभूतं ।८। अधिदैवतं ।९। पञ्चाभिबुद्धयः ।१०। पञ्च कर्मयोनयः ।११। पञ्च वायवः ।१२। पञ्च कर्मात्मानः ।१३। पञ्चपर्वाविद्या ।१४। अष्टाविंशतिधाशक्तिः ।१५। नवधा तुष्टिः ।१६। अष्टधा सिद्धिः ।१७। दशधा मूलिकार्थाः ।१८। अनुग्रहसर्गः ।१९। चतुर्दशविधो भूतसर्गः ।२०। त्रिविधो धातुसंसर्गः ।२१। त्रिविधो बन्धः ।२२। त्रिविधो मोक्षः ।२३। त्रिविधं प्रमाणं ।२४।

त्रिविधं दुःखं ।२५। एतद्याथातथ्यं । एतत्सम्यक् ज्ञात्वा कृतकृत्यः स्यात् न पुनस्त्रिविधेन दुःखेनाभिभूत इति तत्त्वसमासाख्यसांख्यसूत्राणि ॥

No. 4.—"(1) The eight 'producers' *(prakriti)*; (2) the six-"teen 'productions' *(vikára)*; (3) 'Soul' *(purusha)*; (4) the "'triad of qualities' *(traigunya)*; (5) 'emanation' or 'develope-"ment' *(sanchara)*; (6) 're-absorption' or 'dissolution' *(pratisan-"chara)*; (7) the 'ministers of Soul' *(adhyátma)*; (8) the 'pro-"vince of an organ' *(adhibhúta)*; (9) the respective 'presiding "deity' *(adhidaivata)*; (10) the five 'perversities of understand-"ing" *(abhibuddhi)*; (11) the five 'sources of action' *(karmma-"yoni)*; (12) the five 'airs' *(váyu)*; (13) the five 'which consist "of action' (*karmmátma*); (14) 'ignorance' *(avidyá)* under five "divisions; (15) 'disability' (*as'akti*) of twenty-eight kinds; (16) "'acquiescence' or 'indifference' *(tushṭi)* of nine kinds; (17) "'perfectness' *(siddhi)* of eight kinds; (18) the 'radical facts' "*(mulikártha)* of ten kinds; (19) 'benevolent nature,' *(anugra-"ha-sarga)*; (20) 'created existences' *(bhúta-sarga)* of ten des-"criptions; (21) 'parental creation' *(dhátu-sansarga)* of three dis-"criptions; (22) three-fold 'bondage' (*bandha*); (23) three-fold "'liberation' (*moksha*); (24) three-fold 'proof' (*pramáṇa*); (25) "three-fold 'pain' (*du'kha*):— in this consists all actual truth. "He who shall have thoroughly understood this, will have done "all that is to be done. He will not again be obnoxious to the "three sorts of pain."

Such are the Aphorisms of the *Sánkhya,* entitled the 'Compendium of Principles.'

[The commentator then proceeds to dilate on each of the foregoing topics.]

अथ का अष्टौ प्रकृतयः। इत्युच्यते। अव्यक्तं बुद्धिरहंकारःपञ्च तन्मात्राणीत्येता अष्टौ प्रकृतयः ।

No. 5.—Now which are those eight 'producers'? To this it is replied—(1) the 'undiscrete' (*avyakta*); (2) 'intellect' (*buddhi*); (3) 'self-consciousness' (*ahankára*); and (4—8) the five 'subtile rudiments' (*tan-mátra*);— these are the eight 'producers.'

[Each of these eight 'producers' is now taken up in its order.]

तत्राव्यक्तं तावदुच्यते। यथा लोके व्यज्यन्ते घटपटकुटशयनकाद्या न तथा व्यज्यत इत्यव्यक्तं। श्रोत्रादिभिरिन्द्रियैर्न गृह्यते इत्यर्थः। कस्मात्। अनादिमध्यान्तत्वान्निरवयवत्वाच्च। अशब्दमस्पर्शमरूपमव्ययन्तथाच नित्यं रसगन्धवर्जितं। अनादिमध्यं महतः परं ध्रुवं प्रधानमेतत्प्रवदन्ति सूरयः। सूक्ष्ममलिंगमनादिनिधनं तथाप्रसवधर्मि निरवयवमेकमेव हि साधारणमेतदव्यक्तं ।

No. 6.—Now the 'undiscrete' is described. As, in this world, jars, webs, vases, and couches are made manifest, not so is the 'undiscrete':—that is to say—it is not apprehended by the hearing or by any other sense. Why? Because it has neither beginning, middle, nor end; nor is it made up of parts. The inaudible, intangible, invisible, indestructible, and likewise eternal, devoid of savour and odour,—without beginning or middle, anterior in order to mind, firm and chief—thus do the learned designate it. Subtile, devoid of characteristic attributes, unconscious, without beginning or end,—so too whose nature it is to produce, without parts, one only, the common [source of all]—such is the 'undiscrete.'

अव्यक्तस्यामी पर्यायशब्दा भवन्ति । अव्यक्तं । प्रधानं । ब्रह्म । पुरं । ध्रुवं । प्रधानकं । अक्षरं । क्षेत्रं । तमः । प्रसूतमिति ।

No. 7.—Synonymes of the 'undiscrete' are the following—viz: the 'undistinguished,' 'unseparated,' or 'imperceptible' (*avyakta*); the 'chief' (*pradhána*); the 'source of emanation' (*brahma*): the 'receptacle' or 'abode,' (*pura*); the 'permanent' (*dhruva*); the 'chief,' or 'that in which all generated effect is comprehended' (*pradhánaka*); the 'indestructible' (*akshara*); the 'site' or 'field' (*kshetra*); 'darkness' (*tamas*); the 'productive source' (*prasúta*).

[Several of these terms are not, strictly speaking, synonymes, further than as they are all applicable to the 'undiscrete'. They are epithets employed for reasons which may appear in the sequel. A similar remark applies to the various lists of synonymes which will be met with further on.

We now come to the second of the eight 'producers' (No. 5) —viz 'intellect'.]

का बुद्धिरत्रोच्यते । अध्यवसायो बुद्धिः । सो ऽयमध्यवसायो गवादिषु द्रव्येषु यस्मात्प्रतिपत्तिः । एवमेतन्नान्यथा । गौरेवायं नाश्वः । स्थाणुरेवायं न पुरुषः । इत्येषा बुद्धिः ।

No. 8.—What is 'intellect'? To this it is replied—'intellect' is 'ascertainment' (*adhyavasáya*). This it is from which, in regard to a cow or any other thing, there is the determination 'This is so and so, and not otherwise'—'This is a cow, not a horse'—'This is a post, not a man.' Such is 'intellect' or 'understanding.'

[The various aspects under which this faculty is regarded as presenting itself, are next specified.]

अस्यास्तु बुद्धेरष्टौ रूपाणि भवन्ति धर्मो ज्ञानं वैराग्यमैश्वर्यमि-
ति ।

No. 9.—Of this 'intellect' there are eight forms—(1) 'virtue' *(dharma)*; (2) 'knowledge' *(jnyána)*; (3) 'dispassion' *(vairágya)*; (4) superhuman 'power' *(aiswarya)*—[the remaining four being the opposites or negatives of these. See No. 14.]

तच्च धर्मो नामाधर्मविपर्ययः श्रुतिस्मृतिविहितः शिष्टाचारा-
विरुद्धः शुभलक्षणः ।

No. 10.—'Virtue' *(dharma)* is the opposite of 'vice' *(adharma)*; it is what is enjoined in the 'scripture' *(s'ruti)* and in the 'law' *(smriti)*; not opposed to the practice of the pious—of which the symptom is felicity [—prosperity being regarded as the fruit of former virtue, and adversity as that of former vice.]

ज्ञानं नामाज्ञानविपर्ययः । तत्वभावभूतानां सम्बोधः ।

No. 11,—'Knowledge' *(jnyána)* is the opposite of 'ignorance' *(ajnyána)*—an acqaintance with the 'principles' (*tatwa*), the 'forms' of intellect (*bháva*-No. 9.), and the 'elements' (*bhúta*-No 31.)

वैराग्यं नामावैराग्यविपर्ययः । शब्दादिविषयेष्वप्रसक्तिः ।

No. 12.—'Dispassion' *(vairágya)* is the opposite of 'passion' *(avairágya)*:—it consists in not concerning one's self about sounds or any other 'objects of sense' *(vishaya)*.

ऐश्वर्यं नामानैश्वर्यविपर्ययः । अणिमादयो ऽष्टगुणाः । ए-
तानि सात्विकानि चत्वारि ।

No. 13.—Superhuman 'power' *(aiswurya)* is the opposite of 'powerlessness' *(anaiswarya)*; it consists of the eight qualities, [the capacity of assuming a form of the utmost] 'minuteness' *(anímá)* &c.

These four [kinds of 'intellect'—Nos. 10.—13.] are [regarded as] 'partaking of the quality of goodness' (*sátwika*). [See No. 50].

अधर्मोऽज्ञानमवैराग्यमनैश्वर्यमिति । अधर्मो नाम धर्मविपर्ययः । श्रुतिस्मृतिविरुद्धः । शिष्टाचारविरुद्धः । अशुभलक्षणः । अज्ञानं नाम ज्ञानविपर्ययः । तत्त्वभावभूतानामनवबोधः । अवैराग्यं नाम वैराग्यविपर्ययः । शब्दादिविषयेष्वभिनिवेशः । अनैश्वर्यं नाम ऐश्वर्यविपर्ययः । अणिमादिरहितत्वं । एतानि तामसानि चत्वारि ।

No. 14.—'Vice' (*adharma*), 'ignorance' (*ajnyána*), 'subjection to passion' (*avairágya*), and 'powerlessness' (*anaiswarya*), [are next described].

'Vice' is the opposite of 'virtue'—opposed to Scripture and Law—opposed to the practice of the pious—and of which the symptom is adversity. [See No. 10].

'Ignorance' is the opposite of 'knowledge'—the reverse of an acquaintance with the 'principles', the 'forms' of intellect, and the 'elements'. [See No. 11.]

'Subjection to passion' is the opposite of 'dispassion':—it consists in perseveringly concerning one's self about sounds and other objects of sense.

'Powerlessness' is the opposite of superhuman 'power':—it is the being destitute of [the capacity of] 'minuteness' &c.

These four [kinds of 'intellect'] are [regarded as] 'partaking of the quality of Darkness' (*támasa*). [See No. 52].

[What consequences severally appertain to the above-described modifications of 'intellect,' is next stated.]

तत्र धर्मेण निमित्तेनोर्ध्वगमनं। ज्ञानेन निमित्तेन मोक्षः। वैराग्येण निमित्तेन प्रकृतिलयः। ऐश्वर्यनिमित्तेनाप्रतिहतगतिर्भवति। एवमेषा त्वष्टरूपा बुद्धिः परिख्याता।

No. 15.—Through 'virtue,' as a cause, there is 'elevation in the scale of being' (*úrdhwa-gamana)*; through 'knowledge,' as a cause, there is 'liberation' from existence (*moksha*); through 'dispassion,' as a cause, there is 'absorption into nature,' (*prakriti-laya*); through superhuman 'power,' as a cause, there is 'unimpeded movement' [even through solid rocks and the like], (*iapratihata-gati*).

Thus has 'intellect,' in its eight forms [No. 9] been described.

बुद्धेरमी पर्यायशब्दा भवन्ति।

मनो मतिर्महान् ब्रह्मा ख्यातिः प्रज्ञा श्रुतिर्धृतिः। प्रज्ञानसन्ततिः स्मृतिर्धीर्बुद्धिः परिकथ्यते।

No. 16.—The following words are synonymes—[See No. 7]—of 'intellect'—viz: 'mind' (*manas*); 'understanding' (*mati*); the 'great' principle (*mahat*); the 'Creator' *(brahmá)*; 'familiar knowledge' (*khyáti*); 'wisdom' (*prajnyá*); 'intelligence through report' (*s'ruti*); 'resolution' (*dhriti*); a 'train of thought' (*prajnyána-santati*); 'memory' (*smriti*); and 'meditation' (*dhí)*; in such terms is 'intellect' spoken of.

[We now come to the third of the eight 'producers' (No. 5)—viz 'self-consciousness'—that which is implied in a man's employing the pronoun 'I'—a pronoun the employment of which declares the speaker's belief that he possesses an individuality of his own.]

अथाह को ऽहंकार इत्युच्यते । अभिमानो ऽहंकारः । यो ऽयमभिमानः । अहं शब्दे अहं स्पर्शे अहं रूपे अहं रसे । अहं गन्धे अहं स्वामी धनवानहमीश्वरः । अहं भोगी अहं धर्मे ऽभिषक्तो ऽसौ मया हतः । अहं हनिष्ये बलिभिः परैरित्येवमादिकः प्रत्ययो यः सो ऽहंकारः ।

No. 17.—To the question—what is 'self-consciousness'?—it is replied that 'self-consciousness' is a 'conceit' (*abhimána*)—the conceit or fancy that 'I am the embracer in the case of sound' [i. e., 'I hear'], 'I feel,' 'I see,' 'I taste,' 'I am lord,' 'I am rich,' 'I am deity,' 'I enjoy,' 'I am connected with virtue,' 'by *me* was he slain,' 'I shall be slain by powerful enemies:'—such and the like belief is 'self-consciousness.'

[The term *ahankára* (the 'making of an *Ego* or an *I'*), the technical import of which, as remarked by Professor Wilson, is 'the pride or conceit of individuality,'* is rendered, in Mr. Colebrooke's version of the *Sánkhya Káriká,* by the term 'Egotism.' It must be carefully borne in mind that the word 'egotism,' thus employed, is not to carry with it the familiar import of bustling vanity—the feeling which prompts a vain man to be constantly talking about himself:—for, a man who is no 'egotist,' in that familiar sense of the term, is not the less chargeable with *ahan-kára,* if he fancies that his employing the pronoun 'I' at all is not an absurdity. The word, as described by *Váchaspati,* in his commentary on the 24th of the *Kárikás* of *I's'wara Krishṇa,* might signify 'egotism' in the ordinary sense—verging even on 'ego-ism,'—i.e., the belief that 'besides me there is nought else:'—but the significance of *Kapila's* system will perhaps be more clearly dis-

* *Sánkhya Káriká*—p. 91.

cerned, if the technical acceptation of the term, as given by Professor Wilson, be strictly adhered to.]

अहंकारस्यामी पर्यायशब्दाः । अहंकारो वैकारिकस्तैजसो भूतादिः सानुमानो निरनुमानश्चेति ।

No. 18.—The various epithets given to 'self-consciousness' are 'the conceit of individuality' (*ahankára*); the 'modifying' (*vaikárika*); the 'ardent' (*taijasa*); the 'origin of the elements' (*bhútádi*); 'dependent on inference' (*sánumána*); and 'independent of inference' (*niranumána*).

[Of the eight 'producers' (No. 5) we have now to consider the last five—viz., the five 'subtile elements'—the rudiments of what are familiarly called the 'elements.']

अथात्र कानि पञ्च तन्मात्राणीत्युच्यते । अहंकारान्वितानि पञ्च तन्मात्राणि । शब्दतन्मात्रं स्पर्शतन्मात्रं रूपतन्मात्रं रसतन्मात्रं गन्धतन्मात्रञ्चेति पञ्च तन्मात्राणि ।

No. 19.—To the question—what are the five 'subtile elements'?—it is replied:—the five 'subtile elements' are consequents of 'self-consciousness.' The 'subtile element of sound' (*s'abda-tanmátra*); the 'subtile element of tangibility' (*spars'a-tanmátra*); the 'subtile element of colour' (*rúpa-tanmátra*); the 'subtile element of savour' (*rasa-tanmátra*); and the 'subtile element of odour' (*gandha-tanmátra*);—these are the five 'subtile elements.'

["*Tan-mátra* is a compound of *tad*, 'that,' and *mátra*, 'alone;' implying, that in which its own peculiar property resides, without any change or variety." In this respect the 'subtile elements' are held to differ from the gross or derivative elements, the properties of which are various at different times and in respect to different mortals.]

तत्र तावच्छब्दतन्मात्राणि शब्देष्वेवोपलभ्यन्ते । उदात्तानुदात्तस्वरितकम्पितषड्जर्षभगान्धारमध्यमपञ्चमधैवतनिषादादयः शब्दविशेषा उपलभ्यन्ते । तस्माच्छब्दतन्मात्रे ऽविशेषः ।

No. 20.—The 'subtile elements of sound' [like the 'atoms' of the Nyáya, which are separately inappreciable by the senses of men,] are apprehended only in [derivative and gross] 'sounds.' Varieties of 'sound' are apprehended, such as 'acutely accented,' 'gravely accented,' 'circumflexly accented,' and [the notes of the gamut—viz.:] 'C' (*shaḍja*), 'D' (*rishabha*), 'E' (*gándhára*), 'F' (*madhyama*—i. e., the 'middle' note of the scale—corresponding to the 'sub-dominant'*), 'G' (*panchama*—i.e. the 'fifth' note of the scale—corresponding to the 'dominant'), 'A' (*dhaivata*), 'B' (*nisháda*), &c. But there is not hence [i. e., in accordance with the variety in sounds appreciable by mortals] any diversity in the 'subtile element of sound' itself.

---

* It is noticeable that the keynote and those two important notes, the dominant and sub-dominant, have names marking their place in the scale, whilst the other names are unscientific and fantastical. The word *rishabha* means 'a bull,' *gándhára* means 'red lead,' *dhaivata* seems to have no sense elsewhere, and *nisháda* means 'an outcaste.' The keynote—viz., *shaḍ-ja* 'born of six' is said to be so named because it is "supposed to require for its articulation the employment of the tongue, teeth, palate, nose, throat and teeth,"—but this is evidently the conjecture of a grammarian, not of a musician. The writers on music may have given it the name as indicative of the acoustic fact that the ear, though content if the keynote be sounded, demands that, if the other six are sounded in their order, the keynote shall follow (before closing) to complete the octave and to form the cadence. It is "the offspring of (all or any of these) six."

अथ स्पर्शतन्मात्राणि स्पर्शेष्वेवोपलभ्यन्ते। तत्र मृदुकठिनकर्कशपिच्छिलशीतोष्णादयः स्पर्शविशेषा उपलभ्यन्ते। तस्मात् स्पर्शतन्मात्रे ऽविशेषः।

No. 21.—The 'subtile elements of tangibility' are apprehended only in [derivative cases—see No. 20—] of 'tangibility.' In these, varieties of 'tangibility' are apprehended—such as 'soft,' 'hard,' 'rough,' 'slippery,' 'cold,' 'hot,' &c. But there is not hence any diversity in the 'subtile element of tangibility' itself.

रूपतन्मात्राणि रूपेष्वेवोपलभ्यन्ते। तत्र शुक्लरक्तकृष्णहरितपीतहारिद्रमांजिष्ठादयो रूपविशेषा उपलभ्यन्ते। तस्माद्रूपतन्मात्रे ऽविशेषः।

No. 22.—The 'subtile elements of colour' are apprehended only in 'colours.' In these, varieties of 'colour' are apprehended—such as 'white,' 'red,' 'black,' 'green,' 'yellow,' 'turmeric-colour,' 'madder-colour,' &c. But there is not hence any diversity in the 'subtile element of colour' itself.

रसतन्मात्राणि रसेष्वेवोपलभ्यन्ते। तत्र कटुतिक्तकषायक्षारमधुराम्ललवणादयो रसविशेषा उपलभ्यन्ते। तस्माद्रसतन्मात्रे ऽविशेषः।

No. 23.—The 'subtile elements of savour' are apprehended only in 'savours.' In this, varieties of 'savour' are apprehended—such as 'pungent,' 'bitter,' 'astringent,' 'alkaline,' 'sweet,' 'acid,' 'salt,' &c. But there is not hence any diversity in the 'subtile element of savour' itself.

गन्धतन्मात्राणि गन्धे एवोपलभ्यन्ते । तत्र सुरभिरसुरभिश्च गन्धविशेषौ उपलभ्येते । तस्माद्गन्धतन्मात्रे ऽविशेषः । एवमेतत्पञ्चतन्मात्राणि सूचितानि ।

No. 24.—The 'subtile elements of odour' are apprehended only in 'odour.' In this, two varieties of 'odour'—viz., 'fragrance' and 'stench,' are apprehended. But there is not hence any diversity in the 'subtile element of odour' itself.

Thus have the five 'subtile elements' been made known.

अथैषां पर्यायशब्दाः । तन्मात्राणि अविशेषाणि महाभूतानि प्रकृतयो ऽभोग्यानि अणवोऽशान्ताघोरामूढानीति । एवमेता अव्यक्तबुद्ध्यहंकारतन्मात्रसंज्ञिता अष्टौ प्रकृतयो व्याख्याताः । अथ कस्मात्प्रकृतयः । प्रकुर्वन्तीति प्रकृतयः ।

No. 25.—Now the synonymes of these are 'elemental rudiments' (*tan-mátra*); 'unvaried' (*avis'esha*); the 'pervading elements' or 'whence the gross elements proceed' (*mahá-bhúta*); 'producers' (*prakriti*); 'not adapted for [mortal] fruition' (*a-bhogya*); 'atoms' (*aṇu*); 'not soothing' (*as'ánta*); 'not terrific' (*aghora*); 'not stupifying' (*amúḍha*). [These last three names refer to the triad of Qualities—see No. 49]. Thus have the eight producers—viz., the 'undiscrete,' 'intellect,' 'self-cousiousness,' and the five 'subtile elements,' been explained.

Now why are these (No. 5) called 'producers'? It is because they produce [the sixteen 'productions'—see No. 4—which are next to be described.]

अथ ते के षोडश विकारा इत्यत्रोच्यते । एकादशेन्द्रियाणि पञ्च भूतान्येते षोडश विकाराः ।

No. 26.—Now what are those sixteen 'productions?' To this it is replied :—the eleven 'organs' (*indriya*), and the five [derivative or gross] 'elements:'—these are the sixteen 'productions, or 'modifications' [*vikára*].

तत्रेन्द्रियाणि तावदुच्यन्ते । श्रोत्रं त्वक्चक्षुषी जिह्वा घ्राणमिति पञ्च बुद्धीन्द्रियाणि ।

No. 27.—Now the 'organs' are set forth. The 'organ of hearing' (*s'rotra*) ; the 'organ of touch' (*twach*) and the 'organ of sight' (*chakshush*); the 'organ of taste' (*jihwá*); the 'organ of smell' (*ghráṇa*); are the five 'organs of the intellect' (*buddhíndriya*).

(These are called 'organs of the intellect' because their function is that of observation, not, as that of the other organs is, of action.)

श्रोत्रं शब्दविषयं बुध्यते । त्वक् स्पर्शविषयं बुध्यते । चक्षू रूपविषयं बुध्यते । रसना रसविषयं बुध्यते । घ्राणो गन्धविषयं बुध्यते । इति

No. 28.—The 'hearing' apprehends its object 'sound' (*s'abda*). The 'touch' apprehends its object 'tangibility' (*spars'a*). The 'sight' apprehends its object 'colour' (*rúpa*). The 'taste' apprehends its object 'savour' (*rasa*). The 'smell' apprehends its object 'odour' (*gandha*).

वाक् पाणिपादम् पायूपस्थाख्यानि पञ्च कर्मेन्द्रियाणि स्वं स्वं कर्म्म कुर्वन्ति । वाक् वचनमुच्चरति । हस्तौ कर्म कुरुतः । पादौ विहरणम् । पायुर्विसर्गम् । उपस्थम् आनन्दम् । उभयात्मकं मनः स्वसंकल्पविकल्पवृत्ती कुरुते । एवमेकादशेन्द्रियाणि व्याख्यातानि ।

No. 29.—The five 'organs of action' (*karmendriya*), viz., the 'voice' or the 'larynx &c.' (*vák*), the 'hands,' the 'feet,' the 'organ of excretion,' and the 'organ of generation,' perform severally their own function. The 'voice' pronounces words. The 'hands' perform actions. The 'feet' perform locomotion; the 'organ of excretion,' evacuation; and the 'organ of generation,' enjoyment. 'Mind' (*manas*), an organ both of observation and action, performs its appropriate functions of 'resolving' (*sankalpa*) and 'doubting' (*vikalpa*).

Thus have the eleven organs been described.

अथैषां पर्य्यायाः । इन्द्रियाणि करणानि वैकारिकाणि नियतानि पदानि अवधृतानि अणूनि अक्षाणीति ।

No. 30.—Now the synonymes of these are—'organs of sense' (*indriya*); 'instruments' (*karaṇa*); 'changers' (*vaikárika*); 'allotted' (to each mortal) (*niyata*); 'appliances' (*pada*); 'placed under' (the soul) (*avadhrita*); 'subtile' (*aṇu*); 'organs' (*aksha*).

अथ कानि पञ्च महाभूतानीत्यत्रोच्यते । पृथिव्यप्तेजोवाय्वाकाशानीति महाभूतानि ।

No. 31.—Now what are the five 'gross elements' (*mahá-bhúta*)? To this it is replied—'earth,' 'water,' 'light,' 'air,' and ether,' are the 'gross elements.'

तत्र पृथिवी धारणभावेन प्रवर्त्तमाना चतुर्णामुपकारं करोति । आपः जलानि क्लेदनभावेन प्रवर्त्तमानानि चतुर्णामुपकारं कुर्वन्ति । तेजः पाचकभावेन प्रवर्त्तमानं चतुर्णामुपकारं करोति । वायुः शोषणभावेन प्रवर्त्तमानश्चतुर्णा मुपकारं करोति । आकाशं अ-

वकाशदानेन प्रवर्त्तमानं चतुर्णामुपकारं करोति । शब्दस्पर्शरूपरसगन्धवती पञ्चगुणा पृथिवी । शब्दस्पर्शरूपरसवत्यश्चतुर्गुणा आपः । शब्दस्पर्शरूपवत्त्रिगुणं तेजः । शब्दस्पर्शवानिति द्विगुणो वायुः । शब्दवदेकगुणमाकाशम् । एवमाख्यातानि पञ्च महाभूतानि ।

No. 32.—'Earth,' acting in the character of supporter, co-operates with the [other] four [elements, in the production of effects.' 'Water' acting in its character of the 'humid,' co-operates with the other four. 'Light,' acting in the way of 'maturation,' co-operates with the other four. 'Air,' acting in the way of 'siccation,' co-operates with the other four. 'Ether,' acting in the way of giving space, co-operates with the other four.

'Earth' is possessed of five qualities—having 'sound,' 'tangibility,' 'colour,' 'savour,' and 'odour.' 'Water,' possesses 'sound,' 'tangibility,' 'colour,' and 'savour.' 'Light' possesses 'sound,' 'tangibility,' and 'colour.' 'Air' possesses 'sound' and 'tangibility.' 'Ether' has the single quality of 'sound.'

Thus have the 'gross' 'elements' been set forth.

अथैषां पर्यायाः । भूतानि । भूतविशेषाः । विकाराः । आकृतयः । तनवः । विग्रहाः । शान्ताः । घोराः । मूढाः । इत्येते षोडश विकारा व्याख्याताः ।

No. 33.—Now their synonymes—'elements' (*bhúta*), 'varieties of element' (*bhúta-vis'esha*), 'productions' or 'modifications' (*vikára*), 'forms' (*ákriti*), 'minute,' (*tanu*), bodies, (*vigraha*), 'soothing,' 'terrific,' 'stupifying.'

Thus have the sixteen 'productions' or 'modifications' been described.

[The eight 'producers,' and the sixteen 'productions,' or results of the modification of the 'producers,' having been thus described, the third of *Kapila's* aphorisms, in which he announces 'soul,' is next adverted to.]

अथाह कः पुरुषः । इत्युच्यते । पुरुषोऽनादिः सूक्ष्मः सर्वगतश्चेतनोऽगुणो नित्यो द्रष्टा भोक्ताऽकर्त्ता क्षेत्रविदमलोऽप्रसवधर्मीति ।

No. 34.—Now it is asked—what is 'soul'? To this it is replied —'soul' is without beginning, subtile, omnipresent, intelligent, without [the three] qualities [see No. 49], eternal, spectator, enjoyer, not an agent, the knower of body, pure, not producing aught.

अथाह कस्मात्पुरुषः । पुराणात्, पुरि शयनात्, पुरोहितवृत्तित्वाच्च पुरुषः ।

No. 35.—Now it is asked—why [is it called] 'soul' (*purusha*)? Because it is 'ancient' (*puráṇa*) [having been from eternity—see No. 34—]; and because 'it reposes in body' (*puri s'ayate*); and because it is that towards which the 'highest affection' (*puro hita*) is entertained [—seeing that each one loves *self*, if loving nought else—] therefore it is called *purusha*.

अथ कस्मादनादिः । नास्यादिरन्तो मध्यो वा विद्यते इत्यनादिः । कस्मात्सूक्ष्मः । निरवयवत्वादतीन्द्रियत्वात्सूक्ष्मः । कस्मात्सर्वगतः । सर्वमाप्तवाननन्तास्पदो गगनवदस्तीति सर्वगतः । कस्माच्चेतनः । सुखदुःखमोहोपलब्धिमत्त्वात् । कस्मादगुणः । सत्त्वरजस्तमांस्यस्मिन्न सन्त्यतोऽगुणः । कस्मान्नित्यः । अकृतकत्वादनु-

त्याद्यत्वाच्च । कस्माद्द्रष्टा । प्रकृतिविकारानुपलभते इति । कस्माद्भोक्ता । चेतनभावात्सुखदुःखपरिज्ञानात् । कस्मादकर्त्ता । उदासीनत्वादगुणत्वाच्च । कस्मात्क्षेत्रविद् । क्षेत्रेभ्यो गुणान्वेत्ति इति क्षेत्रविद् । अथ कस्मादमलः । शुभाशुभकर्माण्यस्मिन् पुरुषे न सन्तीति अमलः । कस्मादप्रसवधर्मी । निर्बीजत्वात् । न किञ्चिदुत्पादयतीत्यर्थः । एवमेष सांख्यपुरुषो व्याख्यातः ।

No. 36.—Now why is it ['soul'] said to be 'without beginning' [No. 34]? Because it has neither beginning, middle, nor end. Why 'subtile'? From its being without parts, and its transcending the senses. Why 'omnipresent'? Because it comes into relation with all, and its sphere is boundless as the sky. Why 'intelligent'? From its discerning pleasure, pain, and delusion. Why 'without qualities'? Because neither the quality of 'goodness' [No. 49], of 'passion,' nor of 'darkness,' is in it. Why 'eternal'? From its not being made or produced. Why 'spectator'? Because it apprehends the modifications which productive nature undergoes. Why 'enjoyer'? Because it discerns pleasure and pain through its possession of intelligence. Why 'not an agent'? From its being indifferent (*udásína*) and devoid of the 'qualities' [see No. 42.] Why the 'knower of body'? Because through bodies it apprehends the 'qualities.' Why 'pure'? Because in this 'soul' there are neither good actions nor bad. Why 'not wont to produce'? Because it is seedless:—that is to say, it does not give rise to any thing.

Thus has the 'soul' of the *Sánkhya* been described?

अथास्य पुरुषस्य पर्यायाः । पुरुषः । आत्मा । पुमान् । पुंगुणजन्तुजीवः । क्षेत्रज्ञः । नरः । कविः । ब्रह्म । अक्षरः । प्राणः ।

य: । क: । स: । एष: । एवमेतानि पञ्चविंशति तत्वानि व्याख्यातानि । अष्टौ प्रकृतय: षोडश विकारा: पुरुषश्चेति ।

पञ्चविंशतितत्वज्ञो यत्रकुत्राश्रमे रत: ।

जटी शिखी मुण्डी वापि मुच्यते नात्र संशय: ॥

No. 37.—Now the synonymes of this 'soul'—the 'reposer in body' *(purusha)*; 'self' *(átmá)*; 'the male' *(puns)*; 'that which superadds the quality of reason to mere animal life' *(pun-guṇa-jantu-jíva)*; the 'knower of body' *(kshetra-jna)*; the 'man' *(nara)*; the 'poet' *(kavi)*; 'deity' *(brahma)*; the 'indestructible' *akshara)*; 'life' or 'vital air' *(práṇa)*; 'who,' 'who'? 'he,' 'this.'

Thus have the twenty-five 'principles' *(tatwa)* been explained —viz:, the eight 'producers' [No. 5], the sixteen 'productions' [No. 26], and 'soul' [No. 34].

"He who knows the twenty-five principles, whatever order of life he may have entered, and whether he wear matted hair, a top-knot only, or be shaven, he is liberated:—of this there is no doubt."

अत्राह । पुरुष: किं कर्त्ता अकर्त्तेति । यदि कर्त्ता पुरुष: स्यात् शुभान् कुर्य्यात् नतु वृत्तित्रयं ।

No. 38.—Here it is asked—is 'soul' an agent, or not an agent? If 'soul' were an agent, it would do only good actions—it would not adopt the 'triad of habits.'

[What the three 'habits' are, is next stated.]

धर्म्मास्थं सौहित्यं यमनियमनिर्वेरिणं प्रसंख्यानं ज्ञानैश्वर्य्यप्रकाशनमिति सात्विकी वृत्ति: ।

No. 39.—The 'amiable' *(sátwika)* habit consists of virtue,

kindliness, restraint [of the senses], regulation [of the organs], freedom from enmity, correct judgment, the attainment of knowledge and supernatural power [see No. 13.]

रागः क्रोधो लोभः परपरिवादो ऽतिरौद्रता ऽतुष्टिर्विकृताकृतिपारुष्यं प्रख्यातैषातु राजसी वृत्तिः ।

No. 40.—But passion, anger, covetousness, the reproaching of others, extreme sternness, discontent, fierceness shown in change of aspect—this is called the 'passionate' *(rájasa)* habit.

उन्मादमदविषादा नास्तिक्यस्त्रीप्रसंगिता निद्रा आलस्यं नैर्गुण्यमशौचमिति तामसी वृत्तिः ।

No. 41.—Madness, intoxication, lassitude, atheism, addiction to women, drowsiness, sloth, worthlessness, impurity—this is called the 'dark' (*támasa*) habit.

एतद् वृत्तित्रयं दृष्ट्वा लोके गुणानां कर्तृत्वं सिद्धमितिचाकर्त्ता पुरुषः सिद्धो भवति ।

No. 42.—Since we see this triad cf habits in the world, the agency of the 'qualities' [in which these habits originate—see No. 49] is established; and hence 'soul' [the agency being thus accounted for independently of it] is proved to be 'not an agent.'

इमान्गुणान्प्रकृतेर्वर्त्तमानान् रजस्तमोभ्यां विपरीतदर्शनात् । अहं करोमीत्यबुधो ऽभिमन्यते । तृणस्य कुब्जीकरणे ऽप्यनीश्वरः सर्वमिदं मया कृतं ममेदं इतिवदन्नभिमानादबुध उन्मत्तः कर्तृवद्भवति ।

No. 43.—Through 'passion' (No. 51) and 'darkness' (No.

52), through an erroneous view, it (viz., 'soul') foolishly imagines—'I am the agent' in regard to these 'qualities' (No. 49) which belong to nature. Though incompetent even to the crooking of a straw, ('soul' imagines) 'All this was made by me—this is mine :'—thus saying, it, through a vain imagination, foolish, insane, becomes as if it were an agent.

अत्राह ॥ प्रकृतेः क्रियमाणानि गुणैः कर्माणि भागशः ।
अहंकारविमूढात्मा कर्त्ताहमिति मन्यते ॥
अनादित्वान्निर्गुणत्वात्परमात्मायमव्ययः ।
शरीरस्थोऽपि कौन्तेय न करोति न लिप्यते ॥
एवं ॥ प्रकृत्यैवच कर्माणि क्रियमाणानि सर्वशः ।
यः पश्यति तथात्मानमकर्त्तारं स पश्यति ॥

No. 44.—On this subject it is said (in the *Bhagavad Gitá*—Lect. III v. 27.) "Actions are effected by the qualities of nature, according to their shares :—the soul, deluded by the conceit of individuality, imagines 'I am the agent.'"

(And again, Lect. XIII. v. 31.)

"From its being without beginning, and its being devoid of the 'qualities,' this incorruptible supreme Soul, even while remaining in body, neither acts nor is affected."

Also—(Lect. XIII. v. 29).

"Whoso beholds actions as in all respects performed by nature alone, and so too beholds Soul as a non-agent—he indeed sees (aright)."

तत्राह । किमयमेकः पुरुषो बहवो वेत्युच्यते । सुखदुःखमोहसंकरविशुद्धकरणपाटवजन्ममरणकरणानां नानात्वात्पुरुषबहुत्वं सिद्धं लोकाश्रमवर्णभेदाच्च । यद्येकः पुरुषः स्यादेकस्मिन् सुखिनि

सर्व एव सुखिनः स्युः । एकस्मिन् दुःखिनि सर्व एव दुःखिनः स्युः । एकस्मिन् मूढे सर्वे मूढाः स्युः । एकस्मिन् संकीर्णे सर्वे संकीर्णाः स्युः । एकस्मिन् विशुद्धे सर्वे विशुद्धाः स्युः । एकस्मिन् करणपाटवे सर्वेषां करणपाटवं स्यात् । एकस्मिन् जाते सर्वे जायेरन् । एकस्मिन् मृते सर्वे म्रियेरन् । इति नचैक इतश्च बहवः पुरुषाः सिद्धाः । आकृतिगर्भाश्रयभागसंगतिविभागलिंगबहुत्वात् ।

No. 45.—Here the question occurs—is 'soul' one, or many? To this it is replied:—the multiplicity of 'soul' is proved by the diversity of the conditions of pleasure, pain, delusion, mixture of race, purity of race, soundness of organs, birth, and death, and by the difference of the world (heaven, earth, and hell,) and of office, and of caste. If there were only one 'soul,' then, when one is happy, all would be happy; when one is grieved, all would be grieved; when one is deluded, all would be deluded; when one is of mixed race, all would be of mixed race; when one is of pure race, all would be of pure race; when one possesses soundness of organs, all would possess soundness of organs; when one is born, all would be born; when one dies, all would die. Hence 'soul' is not one; and hence multifarious 'souls' are proved to exist—for these possess a multiplicity of distinctive characters in the diversified allotment of form, birth, habitation, fortune, society, and body.

एवं तावत्सांख्याचार्याः कपिलासुरिपञ्चशिखपतञ्जलिप्रभृतयो बहून्पुरुषान्वर्णयन्ति । वेदान्तवादिन आचार्या हरिहरहिरण्यगर्भव्यासादय एकमेवात्मानं वर्णयन्ति ।

No. 46.—Thus [as set forth in No. 45] do the teachers of the

Sánkhya, Kapila, Asuri, Panchas'ikha, Patanjali, &c , describe souls as many. The teachers who speak according to the *Vedánta* [the doctrine derived from the *Vedas,*] viz., Harihara, Hiranya-garbha, Vyása, &c., describe Soul as one only.

कस्मादेवं । तदाह । पुरुष एवेदं । सर्वं यद्भूतं यच्च भाव्यं उता-
मृतत्वस्येशानो यदन्येनातिरोहति । तदेवाग्निस्तदादित्यस्तद्वा-
युस्तच्च चन्द्रमाः । तदेव शुक्रं तद्ब्रह्म तदापः स प्रजापतिः । तदेव
सत्यममृतं स मोक्षः सा परागतिः । तदक्षरं तत्सवितुर्वरेण्यं यस्मा-
त्परं नापरमस्ति किञ्चित् यस्मान्नाणीयो न ज्यायोऽस्ति किञ्चित् ।

No. 47.—Why thus (but one)? He replies. This [universe] is Soul only. [Soul is] all that has been, and that is to be, and the lord of immortality—that which by nought else is overlaid. It alone is fire, it is the sun, it is air, and it is the moon. It alone is pure, it is the vast one, it is the waters, it is the lord of creatures, it alone is the true nectar of immortality, it is liberation, it is the ultimate goal, it is the indestructible, it is the glory of the sun, it is that beyond which there is nothing else, than which there is nothing either more recent or more ancient.

वृक्ष इव स्तब्धो दिवि तिष्ठत्येकस्तेनेदं पूर्णं पुरुषेण सर्वं सर्वतः
पाणिपादं तत्सर्वतोक्षिशिरोमुखं सर्वतः श्रुतिमल्लोके सर्वमावृत्य
तिष्ठति । सर्वेन्द्रियगुणाभासं सर्वेन्द्रियविवर्जितं । सर्वेषां प्रभु-
मीशानं सर्वस्य शरणं महत् । सर्वतः सर्वतत्त्वानि सर्वात्मा सर्व-
सम्भवः । सर्वं निलीयते यस्मिन् तद्ब्रह्म मुनयो विदुः । एक
एव हि भूतात्मा देहे देहे व्यवस्थितः । एकधा बहुधा चैव दृश्य-

ते जलचन्द्रवत् । स हि सर्वेषु भूतेषु स्थावरेषु चरेषु च । वसत्येको महात्मा येन सर्वमिदं ततं । एको ऽयमात्मा जगतां स केन बहुधा कृतः । पृथक् वदन्ति चात्मानं ज्ञानादिकप्रवर्त्तने । ब्राह्मणे कृमिकीटेषु श्वपाके शुनि हस्तिनि । पशुगोदंशमशके समं पश्यन्ति पण्डिताः । एकमेव यथा सूत्रं सुवर्णे वर्त्तते पुनः । मुक्तामणिप्रवालेषु मृण्मये रजते तथा । तद्वद्गोषु मनुष्येषु तद्वद्धस्तिमृगादिषु । एको ऽयमात्मा विज्ञेयः सर्वत्रैव व्यवस्थितः ।

No. 48.—Firm as a tree it remains in the heavens. With that Soul all this is filled everywhere. On all sides are the hands, feet, eyes, heads, and faces of that [Soul-tree]—and, with ears in all directions, it stands embracing all—assuming the aspect of all the organs and qualities, though devoid of all the qualities—the lord and ruler of all—the great refuge of all—that which altogether is all the principles, is every soul, is the source of all—into which all is resolved—the sages regard it as *Brahma.* For only one soul is located in various bodies; as the Moon, though but one, appears many in [many vessels of] water. In all existences, immoveable or locomotive, it dwells—one only—by which all this [universe] was spread out. This soul, of all worlds, is but one:—by *whom* is it made more? Some speak of soul as several—seeing that Knowledge and other mental states are observable [simultaneously—some being happy while others are sad]; but in the Bráhman, the worm, and the insect; in the outcaste, the dog, and the elephant; in goats, cows, gadflies, and gnats, the wise behold the same [single Soul]. Just as a thread may pass through golden beads, and again in like manner through pearls, gems, coral, earthen beads, or silver,—so this Soul is to be regarded as remaining everywhere one—in cows, men, elephants, deer, &c.

अत्राह किं त्रैगुण्यं नाम । उच्यते । सत्त्वरजस्तमांसीति त्रैगुण्यं । त्रिगुणा एव त्रैगुण्यं ।

No. 49.—Now it is asked—what is the 'triad of qualities'? It is replied—the triad of qualities consists of 'Goodness' (*sattwa*), 'Foulness' (*rajas*), and 'Darkness' (*tamas*). By the 'triad of qualities' is meant the 'three qualities.'

सत्त्वं नाम प्रसादलाघवप्रसन्नाभीष्टगतितुष्टितितिक्षासन्तोषादि लक्षणमनन्तभेदं समासतस्सुखात्मकं ।

No. 50.—'Goodness' (*sattwa*) is endlessly diversified, accordingly as it is exemplified in calmness, lightness, complacency, attainment of wishes, kindliness, contentment, patience, joy, and the like. Summarily, it consists of happiness.

रजो नाम शोकतापभेदोद्वेगदोषगमनादिलक्षणमनन्तभेदं समासतो दुःखात्मकं ।

No. 51.—'Foulness' (*rajas*) is endlessly diversified, accordingly as it is exemplified in grief, distress, separation, excitement, anxiety, fault-finding, and the like. Summarily, it consists of pain.

तमो नाम आच्छादनाज्ञानबीभत्सदैन्यगौरवालस्यनिद्राप्रमादादिलक्षणमनन्तभेदं समासतो मोहात्मकं ।

No. 52.—'Darkness' (*tamas*) is endlessly diversified, accordingly as it it is exemplified in envelopement, ignorance, disgust, abjectness, heaviness, sloth, drowsiness, intoxication, and the like.

Summarily, it consists of delusion.

एतावत्त्रैगुण्यं व्याख्यातं ।
सत्त्वं प्रकाशकं विद्याद्रजो विद्यात्प्रवर्त्तकम् ।
तमोऽप्रकाशकं विद्यात् त्रैगुण्यं नाम संज्ञितं ॥

No. 53.—So far (i. e. in Nos. 50, 51, and 52,) has the 'triad of qualities' been expounded.

One should regard 'goodness' as 'illuminating;' one should regard 'foulness' as 'exciting'; one should regard 'darkness' as 'non-illuminating';—such is what is named the 'triad of qualities.'

अत्राह कः संचरः प्रतिसंचरश्च । अत्रोच्यते । उत्पत्तिः संचरः । प्रलयः प्रतिसंचरः । तत्रोत्पत्तिर्नाम ।

अव्यक्तात्प्रागुपदिष्टात्सर्वगतपुरुषेण परेणाधिष्ठिता बुद्धिरुत्पद्यते । अष्टगुणा बुद्धिः । बुद्धेस्तत्त्वादहंकार उत्पद्यते । सोऽहंकारस्त्रिविधो वैकारिकस्तैजसो भूतादिरिति । तत्र वैकारिकादहंकाराद् देवता इन्द्रियाणि चोत्पद्यन्ते । भूतादेस्तन्मात्राणि । तैजसादुभयं । तन्मात्रेभ्यो भूतानीति संचरः ।

No. 54.—The next question is—what is (meant by) 'developement' and 'resolution' (*sanchara* and *pratisanchara*—the 5th and 6th in Kapila's enumeration of topics—No. 6)? To this it is replied—'development' is production :—'reabsorption' (*pratisanchara*) is dissolution. [The order of] 'production' is as follows :—from the 'undiscrete' beforementioned [No. 7], superintended by Soul, which is another [than Nature, and for whose use is the assemblage of sensible objects,] and omnipresent, 'intellect' is produced. 'Intellect' is of eight kinds—[No. 9]. From the principle of 'intellect' 'self-consciousness' [No. 17] is produced. 'Self-consciousness' is of three kinds [No. 18]—the 'modifying,' the 'active,' 'ardent,' or 'urgent,' and the 'origin of the elements.' From the 'modifying self-consciousness' the gods and the senses are produced; from [self-consciousness as] 'the origin of the elements' the 'subtile elements' (No. 19) are produced. From the 'active' both proceed, [for, without the 'active,' both the others are held to be inert]. From the 'subtile elements [are produced] the [gross] 'elements:'—such is [the order of] 'development.'

प्रतिसंचरो नाम भूतानि तन्मात्रेषु लीयन्ते तन्मात्राणीन्द्रियाणि चाहंकारे ऽहंकारो बुद्धौ बुद्धिरव्यक्ते । तदव्यक्तं क्वचिन्न प्रलीयते । कस्मादनुत्पद्यमानत्वात् । प्रकृतिं पुरुषं चैव विद्ध्यनादीत्येवं प्रतिसंचरो व्याख्यातः ।

No. 55.—'Reabsorption' [No. 6] is as follows:—the 'elements' are resolved into the 'subtile elements;' the 'subtile elements' and the 'senses' into 'self-consciousness;' 'self-consciousness' into 'intellect;' 'intellect' into the 'undiscrete.' The 'undiscrete' is nowhere dissolved. Why? Because it was not produced out of anything (into which it might be resolvable). Regard Nature and Soul as being both eternal. Thus has 'reabsorption' been explained.

तत्राह किं तदध्यात्ममधिभूतमधिदैवं चेति । तत्रोच्यते । बुद्धिरध्यात्मं बोधयितव्यमधिभूतं ब्रह्मा तत्राधिदैवतं । अहंकारोऽध्यात्मं मन्तव्यमधिभूतं रुद्रस्तत्राधिदैवतं । मनोऽध्यात्मं संकल्पि-

तव्यमधिभूतं चन्द्रस्तत्राधिदैवतं। श्रोत्रमध्यात्मं श्रोतव्यमधिभूतं आकाशमधिदैवतं। त्वगध्यात्मं स्पर्शयितव्यमधिभूतं वायुस्तत्राधिदैवतं। चक्षुरध्यात्मं द्रष्टव्यमधिभूतं आदित्यस्तत्राधिदैवतं। जिह्वाध्यात्मं रसयितव्यमधिभूतं वरुणस्तत्राधिदैवतं। घ्राणमध्यात्मं घ्रातव्यमधिभूतं पृथ्वी तत्राधिदैवतं। वागध्यात्मं वक्तव्यमधिभूतं वह्निस्तत्राधिदैवतं पाणी अध्यात्मं ग्रहीतव्यमधिभूतं इन्द्रस्तत्राधिदैवतं। पादावध्यात्मं गन्तव्यमधिभूतं विष्णुस्तत्राधिदैवतं। पायुरध्यात्मं उत्स्रष्टव्यमधिभूतं मित्रस्तत्राधिदैवतं। उपस्थमध्यात्मं आनन्दयितव्यमधिभूतं प्रजापतिस्तत्राधिदैवतं। एवमेतत्त्रयोदशविधस्य करणस्याध्यात्ममधिभूतमधिदैवतं।

No. 56.—Now it is asked—what is meant by the 'ministers of soul' [No 6], the 'province of an organ,' and the 'presiding deity?' To this it is replied:—'intellect' is a 'minister of soul;' 'whatever is to be understood' constitutes its 'province;' and its 'presiding deity' is Brahmá. 'Self-consciousness' is a 'minister of soul;' whatever is 'to be believed' constitutes its 'province;' and Rudra is its 'presiding deity.' 'Mind' is a 'minister of soul;' whatever is 'to be resolved on' constitutes its 'province;' the Moon is its 'presiding deity.' The 'hearing' is a 'minister of soul;' whatever is 'to be heard' constitutes its 'province;' the Ether is its 'supernatural presiding power.' The 'touch' is a 'minister of soul;' whatever is 'to be touched' constitutes its 'province;' the air is its 'supernatural presiding power.' The 'sight' is a 'minister of soul;' whatever is 'to be seen' constitutes its 'province;' the sun is its 'presiding deity.' The 'taste' is a 'minister of soul;' whatever is 'to be tasted' constitutes its 'province;' Varuṇa [the god of the waters] is its 'presiding deity.' The 'smell' is a 'minister of soul;' whatever is 'to be smelled' constitutes its 'province;' the Earth is its 'supernatural presiding power.' The 'voice' is a 'minister of soul;' whatever is 'to be uttered' constitutes its 'province;' its 'presiding deity' is either Saraswatí or Fire. The 'hands' are 'ministers of soul;' whatever is 'to be grasped' constitutes their 'province;' Indra is their 'presiding deity'. The feet are 'ministers of soul;' whatever is 'to be gone over' constitutes their 'province;' Vishṇu is their 'presiding deity.' The 'organ of excretion' is a 'minister of soul;' whatever is 'to be excreted' constitutes its 'province;' Mitra is its 'presiding deity'. The 'organ of generation' is a 'minister of soul;' what is 'to be enjoyed' constitutes its 'province;' Prajápati is its 'presiding deity.'

Such, in the case of each of the thirteen kinds of instruments [of the soul], is the respective 'minister,' 'province,' and 'presiding deity'.

तत्त्वानि यो वेदयते यथावद्। गुणस्वरूपाण्यधिदैवतंच। विमुक्तपाप्मा गतदोषसङ्घो। गुणांस्तु भुङ्क्ते न गुणैः स युज्यते।

॥ इति तत्त्ववादः ॥

No. 57.—Whosoever is correctly acquainted with the 'principles' [viz. the 8 'producers', 16 'productions,' and 'soul'], the nature of the 'qualities,' and the 'presiding deities' [No. 56], being liberated from his sins and released from the whole of his defects, enjoys [the various pleasing effects of] the 'qualities,' (while he remains in the world) and is liberated from the 'qualities' (when he attains to final emancipation).

So much for the discussion of the [25] 'principles' (*tattwa*).

अथ कास्ताः पञ्चाभिबुद्धयः । उच्यते । व्यवसायो ऽभिमान इच्छा कर्त्तव्यता क्रियेति । अभिमुखबुद्धिरिदं करणीयं मयेति व्यवसायो बुद्धिक्रिया । आत्मपरात्मस्वरूपप्रत्ययाभिमुखो ऽभिमानो अहंकारो बुद्धेः क्रिया । इच्छा वाञ्छा संकल्पो मनसो बुद्धिक्रिया । शब्दादिविषयेन्द्रियश्रवणादिलक्षणकर्त्तव्यता बुद्धीन्द्रियाणां बुद्धिक्रिया । वचनादिलक्षणबुद्धिक्रिया कर्मेन्द्रियाणां सा क्रियेति । एवमेताः पञ्चाभिबुद्धयो व्याख्याताः ।

No. 58.—Now what are those five 'intelligent functions' (No. 6)? To this it is replied:—'ascertainment' (*adhyavasáya*), 'conceit' (*abhimána*), 'willing' (*ichchhá*), 'adaptability' (*karttavyatá*), and 'action' (*kriyá*). The function of intellect when it decides 'This is to be done by me,' is 'ascertainment' (*adhyavasáya*). That function of the intellect, self-consciousness,—the notion that 'I act'—which fixes on the conceptions of 'self' and 'not-self'—is 'conceit'. The intelligent function of 'mind' is 'willing'—desiring and purposing. The intelligent function of the organs of sense (No. 27) is the 'adaptability' of each sense, such as the hearing, or the like, to its object, such as sound, or the like. The intelligent function of those (organs of action—No. 29—) which are recognised by 'utterance,' and the like, is called 'action'.

Thus have the five 'intelligent functions' been explained.

अथ कास्ताः पञ्च कर्म्मयोनय इत्युच्यते । धृतिः श्रद्धा सुखा ऽविविदिषा विविदिषाच पञ्च कर्म्मयोनयः ।

वाह्यकर्म्माणि संकल्प्य प्रतीतं योऽभिरक्षति ।

तन्निष्ठस्तत्प्रतिष्ठश्च धृतेरेतद्धि लक्षणं ॥
स्वाध्यायो ब्रह्मचर्यञ्च यजनं याजनं तपः ।
दानं प्रतिग्रहो होमः श्रद्धाया लक्षणं स्मृतं ॥
सुखार्थं वस्तु सेवेत विद्याकर्म्मतपांसि च ।
प्रायश्चित्तपरो नित्यं सुखेयं परिकीर्त्तिता ॥

विषयभक्षुमिश्रितान्तः करणत्वमविविदिषा । विविदिषाच ध्यानिनां प्रज्ञानयोनिः ।

एकत्वंच पृथक्त्वंच नित्यंचैवमचेतनं ।
सूक्ष्मसत्कार्य्यमक्षोभ्यं ज्ञेया विविदिषाच सा ॥
कार्य्यकारणक्षयकरी विविदिषा प्राकृतिकी वृत्तिः ।
एवमेताः पंच कर्म्मयोनयो व्याख्याताः ।

No. 59.—Now, what are those five 'sources of action' (No. 6)? To this it is replied:—'firmness,' or 'decision of character' *(dhriti)*, 'faith' *(s'raddhá)*, 'piety' *(sukhá)*, 'indifference about knowledge' *(avividishá)*, and 'desire of knowledge' *(vividishá)*: —these are the five 'sources of action.'

Having resolved on any outward act, he who keeps his purpose, being intent on it, and carrying it into effect,—this [conduct of such a man] furnishes the definition of 'firmness.'

The characters by which 'faith' may be recognised are stated to be the perusal of the Scriptures, the condition of the religious student, sacrificing or causing sacrifices, penance, giving and receiving proper donations, and making oblations.

But he who may addict himself to study, to religious actions, and austerities, being always intent on penances with a view to the obtaining of future enjoyments,—this [conduct of such a one] is called 'piety.'

'Indifference about knowledge' implies that the heart is engrossed with the sweets of sensual objects.

'Desire of knowledge' is the source of the wisdom of the wise.

The unity (of Nature), the severalty (of Nature and Soul), the eternity [of Soul] and its unconsciousness, the subtilty [of Nature], the existence of effect [in its cause—even antecedently to manifestation—as the statue exists in the block of marble—] and the duration (of body even after the attainment of knowledge—see No. 69)—this is to be considered (as constituting the assemblage of matters which form the object of) 'the desire of (true) knowledge'.

अथाद्य के पञ्च वायवः । उच्यते । प्राणोऽपानः समानश्च उदानो व्यान एवच इत्येते वायवः पञ्च शरीरेषु शरीरिणां । तत्र प्राणो नाम वायुर्मुखनासिकाधिष्ठाता प्रणयनात्प्रक्रमणाच्च प्राण इत्यभिधीयते । अपानो नाम वायुर्नाभ्यधिष्ठाता अपनयनादधोगमनाच्चापान इत्यभिधीयते । समानो नाम वायुर्हृदधिष्ठाता समनयनात्समगमनाच्च समान इत्यभिधीयते । उदानो नाम वायुः कण्ठाधिष्ठाता ऊर्द्ध्वगमनादुत्क्रमणाच्चोदान इत्यभिधीयते । व्यानः सर्वव्यापकः । इति पञ्च वायवो व्याख्याताः ।

No. 60.—It is now asked—what are the five 'airs' (No. 6)? To this it is replied:—the five airs, in the bodies of those who have bodies, are those named *práṇa*, *apána*, *samána*, *udána*, and *vyána*. The 'air' called *práṇa* is that which is superintended by the mouth and nose. It is so named because it comprises 'inspiration' (*praṇayana*) and 'expiration' (*prakramaṇa*). [This refers to the process of *respiration*]. The 'air' called *apána* is that which is superintended by the navel. It is so called from its 'taking away' (*apanayana*), and 'going downwards'. [This refers to *flatulence*]. The 'air' called *samána* is superintended by the heart. It is so called from its 'leading and going equably' [neither up nor down—as far as regards the food, to aid in the *digestion* of which is its province]. The 'air' called *udána* is that which is superintended by the throat. It is so named from its ascending and 'going upwards' (*utkramaṇa*). [This refers to the arterial pulsation &c. of the upper members of the body—the throat and head]. The 'air' called *vyána* is the 'pervader' (*vyápaka*) of the whole body. [This refers to pulsation in general and all the other involuntary actions of the system.]

Thus have the five 'airs' been described.

अथाह के ते पञ्च कर्म्मात्मान इत्युच्यते। वैकारिकस्तैजसो भूतादिः सानुमानो निरनुमानश्च। तत्र वैकारिकः शुभकर्म्मकर्त्ता। तैजसोऽशुभकर्म्मकर्त्ता। भूतादिर्निगूढकर्मकर्त्ता। सानुमानः शुभमूढकर्त्ता। निरनुमानोऽशुभमूढकर्त्ताचैव पञ्च कर्मात्मानो व्याख्याताः।

No. 61.—It is now asked—what are those five 'whose nature is action' (No. 6)? To this it is replied:—the 'modifying' (*vaikárika*), the 'ardent' (*taijasa*), the 'origin of the elements' (*bhútádi*), that which is 'associated with inference' (*sánumána*), and that which is 'not associated with inference' (*niranumána*). Among these the 'modifying' [form of 'self-consciousness'—see No. 18—] is the agent in good actions:—the 'ardent' is the agent in actions not good:—the 'origin of the elements' is the producer of things good but obscure:—[self-consciousness] 'associated with inference' is the worker of what is good but foolish:—and that which is 'not associated with inference' is the worker of what is not good and (also) foolish.

Thus have the five been explained, 'whose nature is action.'

अत्राह का सा पञ्चपर्वाऽविद्येति । तमो मोहो महामोहस्तामिस्रोऽन्धतामिस्रश्चेति । तत्र तमोमोहावुभावष्टात्मकौ । महामोहो दशात्मकः । तामिस्रोऽन्धतामिस्रश्चाष्टादशात्मकौ । तमो नामाष्टसु प्रकृतिष्वव्यक्तबुद्ध्यहंकारपंचतन्मात्रसंज्ञितासु अनात्मसु आत्माभिमानस्तम इत्यभिधीयते । मोहो नाम अणिमाद्यष्टैश्वर्यप्राप्तये योऽभिमान उत्पद्यते स मोह इत्यभिधीयते । महामोहो नाम दृष्टानुश्रविकेषु शब्दादिविषयेषु दशसु वृत्तिषु मुक्तोऽहमिति मन्यते स महामोह इत्यभिधीयते । तामिस्रो नामाष्टगुणैश्वर्येऽणिमाद्ये दशविधे च विषये यो द्वेषोऽप्रतिहतस्तयं दुःखमुत्पद्यतेऽसौ तामिस्र इत्यभिधीयते । अन्धतामिस्रो नामाष्टगुणैश्वर्येऽणिमाद्ये दशविधे च विषये सिद्धे मरणकाले यो विषाद उत्पद्यते सोऽन्धतामिस्र इत्यभिधीयते । एवमेषा पञ्चपर्वाऽविद्या द्विषष्टिभेदाऽऽख्याता ।

No. 62.—Here it is asked—what is that 'ignorance'—under five divisions [No. 6]? To this it is replied:—'obscurity' (*tamas*), 'illusion' (*moha*), 'extreme illusion' (*mahámoha*), 'gloom' (*tá-misra*), and 'utter darkness' (*andha-támisra*). Among these, 'obscurity' and 'illusion' are each eightfold. 'Extreme illusion' is tenfold. 'Gloom' and 'utter darkness' are eighteenfold.

'Obscurity' is the conceit that [he will be liberated from transmigration because] soul [merges] into [some one or other of] the eight 'producers,' which are not Soul—viz., those called the 'undiscrete,' 'intellect,' 'self-consciousness,' and the five 'subtile 'elements,'—[the errors in regard to these eight severally making up the eight varieties of 'obscurity']. 'Illusion' is the conceit (of liberation) which arises from the possession of the eight kinds of superhuman power, such as 'minuteness' and the rest (No. 13). 'Extreme illusion' is when one supposes 'I am liberated' through (any one of) the ten modes (supplied by) the objects of sense, viz., sounds, &c., belonging to the seen and to the unseen (or scripture-revealed) world—(i. e. the five as perceived by men and the five as perceived by the gods). 'Gloom' is that unchecked hate (or fierce impatience) in regard to the (possession of the) eight kinds of superhuman power, 'minuteness,' &c., and the ten kinds of objects of sense, which (by preventing liberation) results in the three kinds of pain (incident to corporeal existence.) 'Utter darkness' is the name given to that grief which arises at the time of death, when one is in possession of (any one of) the eight kinds of superhuman power, or of the ten kinds of objects of sense.

Thus has fivefold 'ignorance' (the obstruction to the soul's object of final liberation) in its sixty-two varieties, been declared.

अथाह का सा अष्टविंशतिधा ऽशक्तिरुच्यते । एकादशेन्द्रियवधाः सप्तदश बुद्धिवधाः । एषाष्टविंशतिधा ऽशक्तिरिति । तत्रेन्द्रियवधास्तावदुच्यन्ते । श्रोत्रे बाधिर्यं जिह्वायां जडत्वं त्वचि कुष्ठित्वं चक्षुष्यन्धत्वं नासिकायामघ्राणत्वं वाचि मूकत्वं हस्तयोः कुणित्वं पादयोः पंगुत्वं पाय्विन्द्रिये उदावर्त्तं उपस्थेन्द्रिये क्लैब्यं मनसि उन्माद इत्येकादशेन्द्रियवधाः । सप्तदशबुद्धिवधा नाम विपर्ययास्तुष्टिसिद्धीनां । तुष्टिविपर्ययास्तावदुच्यन्ते ।

No. 63.—It is now asked—what is twenty-eightfold 'disability' (No. 6)? To this it is replied:—the depravity of the eleven organs, and the seventeen injuries of the intellect—these constitute twenty-eightfold 'disability.' Now the defects of the organs are stated:—in the organ of hearing, deafness; in the organ of taste, insensibility; in the organ of touch, leprosy; in the organ of sight, blindness; in the organ of smell, loss of smell; in the organ of utterance, dumbness; in the hands, crippledness; in the feet, lameness; in the organ of excretion, constipation; in the organ of generation, impotence; in the mind, insanity:—such are the defects of the eleven organs. The seventeen 'injuries of the intellect' are the reverse of (the nine kinds of) 'acquiescence' and of (the eight kinds of) 'perfectness.' What is meant by the 'reverse of acquiescence' is next stated.

तत्र नास्ति प्रधानमिति या प्रतिपत्तिरनन्ता । एवं महत्यात्मज्ञाने तामसलीना । तथाहंकारस्यादर्शनमवेद्या । नैव सन्ति तन्मात्राणि भूतकारणानीत्यवृष्टिः । विषयाणामर्जने प्रवृत्तिरसुतारा । रक्षणे तु प्रवृत्तिरसुपारा च । क्षयदोषमदृष्ट्वार्थेषु प्रवृत्तिरसुनेत्रा । भोगासक्तिरसुमरीचिका । हिंसादोषमपश्यतो भोगारम्भोऽनुत्तमाम्भसिका । इति तुष्टिविपर्यया नवधाऽतुष्टयो व्याख्याताः ।

No. 64.—Among these [that are the 'reverse of acquiescence' —No. 66—] that called *anantá* is the belief that there is no such thing as Nature. In like manner, (non-acquiescence) in the notion that Soul consists of Intellect, is that called *támasa-líná.* So, again—the non-recognition of 'self-consciousness' is that called *avedyá.* (The notion that) there are no 'subtile elements,' the causes of the gross elements, is that called *avrishṭi.* The concerning one's self about the acquisition of the objects of sense is that (form of non-acquiescence) called *asutára;* and (the concerning one's self) about their preservation is that called *asupára.* The concerning one's self about property, without regarding the evils of waste, is that called *asunetra.* The addiction to enjoyment is that called *asumaríchiká.* The engaging in enjoyment, on the part of one who does not look to the evils arising from injury (to created beings), is that called *anuttamámbhasiká.*

Thus have the ninefold opposites of acquiescence been explained.

[The technical names here are the opposites of those adverted to in section No. 66.]

अथ सिद्धिविपर्य्ययाः । असिद्धयो ऽष्टौचाभिधीयन्ते । नानात्वं भूतमात्रस्यैकत्वमाविर्भूतमतारमुच्यते । शब्दमात्रश्रवणाद्विपरीतग्रहणमसुतारं । यथा नानात्वज्ञो मुक्त इति श्रुत्वा विपरीतं प्रतिपन्नो नानात्वज्ञो ह्यमुक्त इति । अध्ययनश्रवणाभिनिविष्टस्यापि जडत्वादसच्छास्त्रोपहतबुद्धित्वाद्वा पञ्चविंशतितत्त्वज्ञानसिद्धिर्न भवति तदा ऽतारतारं तदज्ञानं । कस्यचिदाध्यात्मिकेन दुःखेनाभिभूतस्यापि संसारेऽनुद्वेगादजिज्ञासोर्न ज्ञानं प्रमोदं । एवमप्रमुदिताप्रमोदमानयोरन्योन्ययोर्द्वयमपरं द्रष्टव्यं । सुहृदुपदिष्टे ऽप्यनिश्चयबुद्धेरज्ञानमरम्यं । असम्यग्वचनादथवा पराङ्मुखे गुरौ दुर्भाग्यस्य ज्ञानासिद्धिस्तदज्ञानमसत्प्रमुदितमिति । एवमेते सिद्धिविपर्य्यया असिद्धयो अष्टौ व्याख्याताः । एवमेषाष्टाविंशतिधा ऽशक्तिराख्याता ।

No. 65.—Now (as regards) the 'opposites' of perfectness. These are called also the eight 'imperfections' (*asiddhi*). When the diversity (of the various principles from which the creation proceeds) appears as the unity of the mere (phenomenal) creation —this (imperfect view of the truth) is called *atára*. After hearing the words merely (of a competent instructor), the adoption of the contrary is that called *asutára* :—as when, having heard that 'he who acknowledges the various principles is liberated,' one determines that it is the reverse—viz., that 'he who acknowledges the various principles is *not* liberated.' When a person, even though intent on studying and hearing, through obtuseness or from his intellect's being impaired by unsound doctrine, does not attain to a perfect knowledge of the twenty-five principles, then his ignorance is called *atáratára*. To another, who, though oppressed by the pain inseparable from body and mind, yet, from feeling no anxiety about transmigration, entertains no curiosity, knowledge is no 'delight' (*pramoda*). Analogously are the next two to be regarded —viz., (the forms of 'imperfection' termed—as the opposites of the corresponding two forms of 'perfectness' in No. 67—) *apramudita* and *apramodamána*. Ignorance that arises from the not arriving at certain knowledge even on being instructed by a friend, is that called *arasya*. When, from his preceptor's disregarding him, or not instructing him correctly, an unfortunate man does not attain to knowledge, his ignorance is called *asatpramudita*.

Thus have those 'opposites of perfectness,' the eight imperfections, been explained. [The technical names are the opposites of those adverted to in section No. 67.]

Thus have the twenty-eight kinds of 'disability' [No. 63] been explained.

अथाद्य का सा नवधा तुष्टिरचोच्यते । प्रकृतिं परमात्मत्वेन

परिकल्प्य परितुष्टे माध्यस्थ्यं लभते तस्य तुष्टेर्या सा तामि-
कीसंज्ञाम्भ इति। अपरो बुद्धिं परमात्मत्वेन प्रतिपद्य परितुष्टस्य
तुष्टेः सलिला इति संज्ञा। अन्यो ऽहंकारं परमात्मत्वेनाभ्युपगम्य प-
रितुष्टस्य तुष्टेरोघ इति संज्ञा। इतरस्तन्मात्राणि अभोग्याख्यानि
परमात्मत्वेन विनिश्चित्य परितुष्टस्तस्य तुष्टेः वृष्टिरिति संज्ञा।
एवं आध्यात्मिकाश्चतस्रस्तुष्टयो भवन्ति। चतसृष्वपि तुष्टिषु ना-
स्ति मोक्षस्तत्वज्ञानस्यासम्भवात्। वाह्या अर्थार्जनरक्षणक्षयसंग
हिंसादिदोषदर्शनाद्विषयोपरमे पञ्च तुष्टयो भवन्ति। अर्थाना-
मर्जने दोषदर्शनात्तुष्टः प्रव्रजितस्यापि नास्ति मोक्षस्तत्वज्ञानाभा-
वात् सा पञ्चमी तुष्टिः सुतारेत्यभिधीयते। अन्यो ऽर्थानां रक्षणे
दोषदर्शनात्तुष्टः प्रव्रजितस्यापि नास्ति मोक्षस्तत्त्वज्ञानाभावात् सा
षष्ठी तुष्टिः सुपारेत्युच्यते। अन्यो ऽर्थानां क्षये दोषदर्शनात्तुष्टः प्रव्र-
जित स्यापि नास्ति मोक्षस्तत्वज्ञानाभावात् सा सप्तमी तुष्टिः सुने-
त्रेत्यभिधीयते। अन्यो ऽर्थानां संगदोषदर्शनान्निवृत्तस्तुष्टः प्रव्रजित-
स्यापि नास्ति मोक्षस्तत्वज्ञानाभावात् सा ऽष्टमी तुष्टिः सुमरीचि-
केत्यभिधीयते। अन्यो भूतानामर्थनिमित्तहिंसादिदोषदर्शनान्निवृ-
त्तस्तुष्टः प्रव्रजितस्यापि नास्ति मोक्षस्तत्वज्ञानाभावात् सा नवमी
तुष्टिरुत्तमा सात्विकीत्यभिधीयते। इत्येता नव तुष्टयो व्याख्याताः।

No. 66.—Now it is asked—what is ninefold 'acquiescence' [No. 6]? To this it is replied:—having supposed that Nature is Soul, a man contentedly betakes himself to indifference:—the technical [or slang] name of his indifference is *ambhas,* [the ordinary sense of which word is 'water']. Another, having satisfied himself that 'intellect' is Soul, is contented. The technical name of his 'acquiescence' is *salila* 'water.' Another, having come to the conclusion that 'self-consciousness' is Soul, is contented. The technical name of his 'acquiescence' is *ogha* 'quantity.' Another, having decided that the 'subtile elements,' those called the 'unfitted for [mortal] fruition' [No. 25] are Soul, is contented. The technical name of his 'acquiescence' is *vrishṭi* 'rain.' Such are the four 'internal' or 'spiritual' (*ádhyátmika*) kinds of 'acquiescence.' Where [together or separately] those four kinds of acquiescence exist, liberation does not take place—from the inconsistency [of such sentiments] with a knowledge of the principles.

The five 'external' (*váhya*) kinds of 'acquiescence' consist in abstaining from [the enjoyment of the five] objects of sense, [such abstinence proceeding] from observation of the evils of acquiring, preserving, waste, attachment [to sensual pleasures], and injuriousness. A man is acquiescent (and abstinent) from observation of the evils attendant on the acquiring of property; but his liberation—even though he be an ascetic—does not take place, because of the (quite possibly concurrent, and here assumed,) absence of a knowledge of the principles. This fifth kind of 'acquiescence' is (technically) named *sutára.* Another is acquiescent from observation of the evils attendant on the preserving of property; but his liberation—even though he be an ascetic—in the absence of a knowledge of the principles, does not take place. This sixth kind of 'acquiescence' is (technically) named *supárá.* Another is acquiescent from observation of the evils of the waste of property; but his liberation—even though he be an ascetic—in the absence of a knowledge of the principles, does not take place. This seventh kind of 'acquiescence' is (technically) named *sunetra* ('a beautiful eye'). Another is acquiescent from observation of the evils attendant on attachment (to sensual pleasures)—but his liberation—even though he be an ascetic—in the absence of a knowledge of the principles, does not take place. This eighth kind of 'acquiescence' is (technically) named *sumaríchiká.* Another is acquiescent, and abstains from worldly acts, from observation of the evils in the shape of injury, &c., to created beings on account of property—but his liberation—even though he be an ascetic—in the absence of a knowledge of the principles, does not take place. This ninth kind of 'acquiescence' is (technically) named *anuttamá* ('best'), or *sátwikí* ('amiable').

Thus have these nine kinds of acquiescence been explained.

अत्राह का ऽष्टौ सिद्धय इत्यत्रोच्यते । यदूहेन ज्ञानमुत्पद्यते तत्त्वभावभूतेषु सा प्रथमा सिद्धिस्तारेत्यभिधीयते । यच्छब्दमात्रेण ज्ञानमुत्पद्यते तत्त्वभावभूतेषु सा द्वितीया सिद्धिः सुतारेत्यभिधीयते । यदध्ययनेन ज्ञानमुत्पद्यते तत्वभावभूतेषु सा तृतीया सिद्धिस्तारयन्तीत्यभिधीयते । यदाध्यात्मिकस्य दुःखस्यापनोदनं कृत्वा ज्ञानमुत्पद्यते तत्वभावभुतेषु सा चतुर्थी सिद्धिः प्रमोदेत्यभिधीयते । यदाधिभौतिकस्य दुःखस्यापनोदं कृत्वा ज्ञानमुत्पद्यते तत्वभावभूतेषु सा पञ्चमी सिद्धिः प्रमोदितेत्यभिधीयते । यदाधिदैवतस्य दुःखस्यापनोदं कृत्वा ज्ञानमुत्पद्यते तत्वभावभूतेषु सा षष्ठी सिद्धिः प्रमोदमानेत्यभिधीयते । यत्स्निग्धसंसर्गाध्यपायाज्ज्ञानमुत्पद्यते तत्वभावभूतेषु सा सप्तमी सिद्धिः रम्यकेत्यभिधीय-

ते। यत्परिचर्य्यादानेन ज्ञानमुत्पद्यते तत्त्वभावभूतेषु परितोषिते गुरौ साष्टमी सिद्धिः सत्प्रमुदितेत्यभिधीयते। इत्येता अष्टसिद्धयो व्याख्याताः।

No. 67.—Now it is asked—what are the eight kinds of 'perfectness' (No. 6)? To this it is replied:—the knowledge which arises from reasoning, in regard to the principles (No. 57), the conditions of intellect (No. 9), and the elemental creation (No. 72)—this, the first kind of 'perfectness,' is (technically) named *tára.* The knowledge, in regard to the principles, the conditions of intellect, and the elemental creation, which arises from hearing alone—this second kind of 'perfectness' is (technically) named *sutára.* The knowledge, in regard to the principles, the conditions of intellect, and elemental creation, which arises from study,—this third kind of 'perfectness' is (technically) named *tárayantí.* The knowledge, in regard to the principles, the conditions of intellect, and the elemental creation, which arises on effecting the removal of internal pain,—this fourth kind of 'perfectness' is (technically) named *pramoda* ('delight'). The knowledge, in regard to the principles, the conditions of intellect, and the elemental creation, which arises on effecting the removal of external pain—this fifth kind of 'perfectness' is (technically) named *pramodita* ('delighted'). The knowledge, in regard to the principles, the conditions of intellect, and the elemental creation, which arises on effecting the removal of pain occasioned by something superhuman—this sixth kind of 'perfectness' is (technically) named *pramodamána.* The knowledge, in regard to the principles, the conditions of intellect, and the elemental creation, which arises from continuance of association with amiable persons,—this seventh kind of 'perfectness' is (technically) named *ramyaká.* The knowledge, in regard to the principles, the conditions of intellect, and the elemental creation, when a teacher is propitiated by giving him veneration, —this eighth kind of 'perfectness' is (technically) named *satpramudita.*

Thus have these eight kinds of 'perfectness' been explained.

अत्राह के दश मूलिकार्था इत्यत्रोच्यते । अस्तित्वमेकत्वमथार्थवत्त्वं परार्थमन्यत्वमकर्तृता च योगो वियोगो बहवः पुमांसः स्थितिः शरीरस्य विशेषवृत्तिः । इत्येते दश मूलिकार्थाः ।

No. 68.—Now it is asked—what are the ten 'radical facts' (No. 6)? To this it is replied—the existence (of 'Soul' and of 'Nature'); the singleness (of Nature); its objectiveness; its subservience; the distinctness (of Soul from Nature); and the inertness (of Soul); the union (of Soul and Nature); the separation (of Soul from its corporeal frame); the peculiar habit of body—its durability (after it ought to have disappeared).

Such are the ten 'radical facts.'

संघातपरार्थत्वादिति पुरुषास्तित्वं सिद्धं । भेदानां परिमाणात्कारणमस्त्यव्यक्तमिति पर्य्यायद्वयेन प्रधानस्यास्तित्वं सिद्धं । हेतुमदनित्यमित्येकत्वं सिद्धं । प्रीत्यप्रीतिविषादात्मकादय इत्यर्थवत्त्वं सिद्धं । नानाविधैरुपायैरिति परार्थत्वं सिद्धं । त्रिगुणमविवेकिविषय इत्यन्यत्वं सिद्धं । तस्माच्च विपर्य्ययादित्यकर्तृत्वं सिद्धं । पुरुषस्य दर्शनार्थं कैवल्यार्थं तथा प्रधानस्यापीति योगः सिद्धः । प्राप्ते शरीरभेदे चरितार्थत्वादिति वियोगसिद्धिः । जन्ममरणकरणानामिति पुरुषबहुत्वं सिद्धं । चक्रभ्रमवदिति विशेषवृत्तिः सिद्धा ।

एते दश मूलिकार्था व्याख्याताः ।

No. 69.—'Since the assemblage of sensible objects is for another's use,' the existence of Soul is established. The existence of Nature is established by the pair in order—(of antecedent and consequent)—viz., that 'since specific objects are finite,' therefore 'there is a general cause which is undiscrete'. Since 'what is causable is inconstant (and multitudinous), &c.,' the singleness (of Nature which is not caused by aught) is established. Since 'these (meaning the Qualities) consist in pleasure, pain, and dulness, &c.,' (see the XIIth of the Memorial Verses of the Sánkhya—) the objectiveness (of Nature) is established. Since 'by manifold means (Nature, without benefit to herself, accomplishes the wish of Soul,)' the subserviency (of Nature) is established. Since 'it (the 'undiscrete,' as well as its modifications) has the three qualities, is indiscriminative, objective, &c.,' the distinctness (of Soul, which is, in all these respects, the reverse,) is established. 'From the contrast' (shown to exist between active Nature and Soul) the inertness (of Soul) is established. 'For the Soul's contemplation of nature, and for its abstraction, &c.'—thus is the union (of the two) established. Since 'separation (of the Soul) from the body takes place, when the object is accomplished,' the separation of the two is established. Since 'of birth, death, and the instruments of life, (the allotment is severally diverse),' the multiplicity of Soul is established. Since it is 'like the whirling of the potter's wheel, (after the impulse that set it in motion has been discontinued),' the peculiar habit (of body, which continues, till death, to invest the soul even of him who has attained to perfect knowledge,) is established.

Thus have the ten 'radical facts' been explained.

सप्तदशानां प्रागुपदिष्टानाञ्च पञ्चाशत् प्रत्यया एतेच षष्टि

पदार्थाः षष्टितन्त्रमित्युच्यते ।

No. 70.—The fifty intellectual modifications consisting of the seventeen (enumerated in Nos. 64 and 65) and of those (thirty three) previously exhibited (in Nos. 62 and 63), together with these (ten 'radical facts'—No. 69—) make up the sixty topics called the 'System of Sixty.'

अत्राह कोऽनुग्रहसर्गः । अत्रोच्यते । वाह्यानां पञ्चतन्मात्रेभ्यस्तोत्पत्त्यानुग्रहसर्गः । मानोत्पत्तेराधारवर्ज्जितानुत्पन्नान्दृष्ट्वा तेभ्यस्तन्मात्रेभ्यो ऽनुग्रहसर्गमसृजद्ब्रह्मा ।

No. 71.—Now it is asked—what is 'benevolent creation' (No. 6)? To this it is replied:—'benevolent creation' consists in the production of external objects from the five 'subtile elements.' (As it is said) 'Brahmá, perceiving these (senses, &c.) produced from thought (—see No. 19) to be destitute of a sphere of action, created, from these 'subtile elements,' this 'benevolent creation.'

अत्राह कश्चतुर्दशविधो भूतसर्ग इत्यत्रोच्यते । अष्टविकल्पो दैवः पैशाचो राक्षसो याक्षो गान्धर्व ऐन्द्रः प्राजापत्यो ब्राह्म इत्यष्टौ देवयोनयः । पञ्चधा तिर्यग्योनिश्च पशुपक्षिमृगसरीसृपस्थावरान्तेति । मानुष्यकश्चैकविधं ब्राह्मणादि चाण्डालान्तं । गवादि मूषकान्तं पशवः । सिंहादि शृगालान्तं मृगाः । गरुडादि मशकान्ताः पक्षिणः । शेषादि कीटान्ताः सरीसृपाः । पारिजातादि तृणान्ताः स्थावराः । इति तिर्यग्योनिश्च पञ्चधा भवति । समासतो ऽयं त्रिधा सर्गः । एतत्संसा-

रमण्डलमुक्तं ।

No. 72.—Now it is asked—what is the fourteenfold 'elemental creation' (No. 6)? To this it is replied:—the divine kind is of eight sorts—that of hobgoblins, of titans, of attendants on the god of riches, of celestial quiristers, of demigods, of divine sages, of the planetary regents, and of the supreme deities. Such are the eight families of divinities. The grovelling kind is fivefold—that of domestic animals, winged animals, wild animals, reptiles, and, lastly, of fixed things. Mankind is single in its class—beginning with the Bráhmaṉ, and ending with the Cháṇḍála. Domestic animals, beginning with the cow, end with the mouse. Wild animals, beginning with the lion, end with the jackal. Winged animals, beginning with the bird of Vishṇu (or the adjutant), end with the gnat. Reptiles, beginning with the World-snake, end with the worm. Fixed things, beginning with the tree of Paradise, end with grass. Thus is the grovelling kind five-fold. Compendiously, this (elemental) creation is threefold—(viz.,—divine, human, and grovelling—and, thus viewed, it supplies the 21st topic in Kapila's enumeration—see No. 6.) All this constitutes what is called the mundane orb.

अथाह कतिविधो बन्धः । इत्यत्रोच्यते । प्रकृतिबन्धो वैकारिकबन्धो दक्षिणाबन्धश्चेति । तत्र प्रकृतिबन्धो नामाष्टौ प्रकृतयस्ताः परत्वेनाभिमन्यमानस्य प्रकृतिलयः प्रकृतिबन्ध इत्युच्यते । तत्र वैकारिकबन्धो नाम प्रव्रजितानां लौकिकानां वैकारिकैरिन्द्रियैर्वशीकृतानां शब्दादिविषये प्रसक्तानामजितेन्द्रियाणामज्ञानिनां काममोहितानां वैकारिकबन्ध इत्युच्यते । दक्षिणाबन्धो नाम गृहस्थब्रह्मचारिभिक्षुवैखानसानां काममोहोपहतचेतसामभि-

मानपूर्विकां दक्षिणां प्रयच्छतां दक्षिणाबन्ध इत्युच्यते । इति त्रि-विधो बन्धो व्याख्यातः । उक्तञ्च प्राकृतेनतु बन्धेन तथा वैकारि-केणच । दक्षिणाभिस्तृतीयेन बन्धो ऽयञ्च निगद्यते ॥

No. 73. —Now it is asked—what is threefold 'bondage' (No. 6)? To this it is replied:—the bondage of the 'producers,' that of the 'modifications,' and that of 'ritual observance.' And first of the 'bondage of the producers:'—this is the name given to the 'absorption into nature' (No. 15.) of him who imagines that (any of) the eight 'producers' constitute Soul. The 'bondage of the modifications' is the name given to that (which opposes the liberation) of those wordly devotees who are in the power of the 'modifications' of nature (No. 26), such as the senses—who are devoted to objects of sense, such as sounds, &c.,—who have not their organs in subjection—who are ignorant, and deluded by passion. The 'bondage of ritual' is the name given to that (which opposes the liberation) of those who, whether householders, students, mendicants, or anchorets, with minds vitiated by passion and delusion, bestow (on Bráhmans, upon solemn or sacrificial occasions,) gifts prompted by conceit.

Thus has threefold 'bondage' been explained. And it is said—"Bondage is spoken of by the title of 'bondage through nature'—'bondage through nature's modifications'—and, thirdly, as that 'through gifts.'"

तत्राह कस्त्रिविधो मोक्षः । ज्ञानोद्रेकादिन्द्रियरागोपशमात्कृत्स्न-क्षयाच्चेति । ज्ञानोद्रेकादिन्द्रियरागोपशमात्स्वधर्म्माधर्म्मक्षयो भवति धर्म्माधर्म्मक्षयाच्च कैवल्यमिति । उक्तञ्च । आदौहि मोक्षो ज्ञानेन

द्वितीयो रागसंक्षयात्। कृत्स्नक्षयात्तृतीयस्तु व्याख्यातं मोक्ष-लक्षणं ॥

No. 74.—Here it is asked—what is threefold 'liberation' (No. 6)?—It is (1) from the increase of knowledge, (2) from the subduing of the senses and passions, and (3) from the destruction of the whole. From the increase of knowledge and the subduing of the senses and passions, there results the destruction both of merit and demerit, and, from the destruction of merit and demerit, (liberation in the shape of) 'singleness' (*kaivalya*). And it is said—"The first liberation is (gained) by knowledge; the second, from the destruction of passion; and the third, from the destruction of all:—such are the characters of liberation."

किं त्रिविधं प्रमाणमित्युच्यते। दृष्टमनुमानमाप्तवचनञ्चेति। एत-त्त्रिविधं प्रमाणं।

No. 75.—What is threefold 'Proof' (No. 6)? To this it is replied:—'perception,' 'inference,' and 'right affirmation'—this is threefold 'proof.'

दृष्टं तावद्व्याख्यायते। यावदिन्द्रियाणां पञ्चेन्द्रियार्थाः प्रत्यक्षा एव दृष्टं।

No. 76.—'Perception' (*drishṭa*) is now described. Whenever the five objects of the senses are present to the senses, there is 'perception.'

अनुमानं प्रमाणं लिङ्गदर्शने जायमानं ज्ञानं। यथा मेघोदये वृष्टिः साध्यते। बलाकादिभिः सलिलं। धूमेनाग्निः। परमिद-मनुमानं।

No. 77.—The proof called 'inference' is knowledge arising on the recognition of a 'sign' (*linga*). For example—by the rising of clouds (regarded as a sign of approaching rain) rain is proved (to be approaching):—by cranes and the like (regarded as a sign attendant on the sheets of water which they frequent) water (is proved to be in the neighbourhood of the place where the cranes are seen). By smoke (regarded as a sign of fire) fire (is proved to exist where the smoke originates):—this is the third kind of inference.

प्रत्यक्षेणानुमानेन वा यो ऽर्थो न साध्यते स आप्तवचनात्साध्यते । यथेन्द्रो देवानां राजा । उत्तराः कुरवः । सौवर्णो मेरुः । स्वर्गे ऽप्सरस इति । ते इन्द्रादयः प्रत्यक्षानुमानासाध्याश्च वशिष्टादयो मुनयो वदन्ति । सन्तीन्द्रादयः । आगमो ऽप्यस्ति । स्वकर्म्मण्यभियुक्तो यो रागद्वेषविवर्जितः । ज्ञानवान् शीलसम्पन्न आप्तो ज्ञेयस्तु तादृशः । एवमेतत्त्रिविधं प्रमाणमभिहितं ।

No. 78.—A fact which is not established by 'perception' or by 'inference,' is established (when it is established) by 'right affirmation'. Such matters (not proveable either by perception or by inference) are (the existence of) Indra the king of the gods, the northern *Kurus,* the golden mountain *Meru,* the nymphs in Paradise. These—Indra, &c.,—not proveable either by perception or by inference, the sages, such as Vas′ishṭa declare—saying "Indra &c. *do* exist." There is also the Scripture (—which is an authority sufficient to establish such points).

"He who is assiduous in his own duties, devoid of passion and malice, intelligent, and virtuous—such a one is to be held 'worthy' (to be received as an authority in regard to matters not demonstrable by perception or by inference)."

Thus has 'threefold proof' been declared.

अथाह तेन त्रिविधेन प्रमाणेन किं साध्यते। अत्रोच्यते। यथा लोके मानेन प्रस्थादिभिर्धान्यानि मीयन्ते तुलयाचन्दनादीनि द्रव्याणि एवमनेन तत्त्वभावभूतानि प्रमीयन्ते।

No. 79.—Now it is asked—what is established by this 'threefold proof'? To this it is replied:—As, in common life, things are estimated by means of a measure—grain and the like by means of such (measures of capacity) as a *prastha,* and sandal &c. by means of weights—so by means of this (apparatus of 'perception,' 'inference,' and 'right affirmation'), the 'principles,' the 'modifications of intellect,' and the 'elemental creation,' [—see No. 67—] are accurately determined [*pramíyante*—whence their name of *pramána* 'proof.']

त्रिविधेन दुःखेनाभिभूतो ब्राह्मणः कपिलमहर्षिं शरणमुपागतः। अत्राह किं त्रिविधं दुःखमित्यत्रोच्यते। आध्यात्मिकमाधिभौतिकमाधिदैविकमिति।

No. 80.—"Oppressed by 'threefold pain,' the Bráhman had recourse to the great sage Kapila"—[see No. 5]—so the question arises—what is 'threefold pain'? To this it is replied—'natural and inseparable' (*ádhyátmika*); 'natural and extrinsic' (*ádhibhautika*); and 'non-natural or superhuman' (*ádhidaivika*).

तत्राध्यात्मिकं द्विविधं शारीरं मानसञ्चेति। शरीरे भवं शारीरं। मनसि भवं मानसमिति। तत्र शारीरं नाम वातपित्तश्लेष्मणां वैषम्याद् दुःखमुत्पद्यते। ज्वरातीसारविसूचिकामूर्च्छादिकं तच्छारीरमुच्यते। कामक्रोधलोभमोहमदेर्ष्यादिकं प्रियवियोगाप्रियसंयोगादिकं तन्मानसमित्युच्यते।

No. 81.—Pain 'natural and inseparable' [No. 80] is of two kinds, corporeal and mental. 'Corporeal' means residing in the body; 'mental' means residing in the mind. Pain, arising from disorder of the wind, bile, or phlegm, and taking the form of fever, flux, cholera, swooning, &c., is called 'corporeal'. Desire, anger, covetousness, folly, madness, envy, &c.,—privation of what is liked and approximation of what is disliked—this is called 'mental' [pain or evil.]

[The pain called *ádhyátmika* is that which arises from the things called *adhyátma*—see No. 56].

अधिभूतेभ्यो भवं आधिभौतिकं । मानुषपशुमृगसरीसृपस्थाव-
रेभ्यो दुःखमुत्पद्यते तदाधिभौतिकं ।

No. 82.—What arises from an object of sense (*adhibúta*—see No. 56)—is called *ádhibhautika* ('natural and extrinsic'). Pain is 'natural and extrinsic' which arises from men, cattle, wild beasts, reptiles, or things that do not move.

अधिदेवेभ्यो जातं आधिदैविकं । शीतोष्णवातवर्षाशनिपाता-
दिनिमित्तं यद् दुःखमुत्पद्यते तदाधिदैविकं ।

No. 83.—What arises from a supernatural agent (*adhidaiva*—see No. 56)—is called *ádhidaivika* ('non-natural' or 'superhuman'). Of this description is pain which arises from cold, heat, wind, rain, thunderbolts, and the like.

अनेन त्रिविधेन दुःखेनाभिभूतस्य ब्राह्मणस्य जिज्ञासोत्पन्ना ।
ज्ञातुमिच्छा जिज्ञासा यथा तृषितस्य पानीयं पातुमिच्छा पिपासा ।

No. 84.—[As stated at the outset—in the mind] of the Bráhman, oppressed by the three kinds of pain, there arose 'a desire to know'—such is the meaning of the word *jijnásá* (the desiderative noun from *jná* 'to know'), just as *pipásá* (from *pá* 'to drink') means the desire of a thirsty man to drink water.

एतत्समासनिश्श्रेयसं। एतज्ज्ञात्वा पुनर्जन्म न स्यादिति। एवं महर्षेर्विज्ञानं कपिलस्य महात्मनः। अनुष्टुप्छन्दसाचात्र ज्ञेयं श्लोकशतत्रयं। इति श्री तत्त्वसमासाख्यसूत्रवृत्तिः समाप्ता। शुभमस्तु॥

No. 85.—This is saving knowledge (derived) from the compendium (of principles laid down by KAPILA.) Having known this, there will be no further transmigration. Such is the doctrine of the magnanimous great sage Kapila.

It is to be observed that there are in this treatise (as much as, three hundred couplets of the *Anushṭhubh* metre.

Thus concludes the comment on the aphorisms called 'The Compendium of Principles.'

86.—Of the name *Sánkhya,* which the philosophical system of KAPILA bears, two explanations are given. According to the one explanation, the system is so named, from the word *sankhyá* 'number,'—"because it observes precision of reckoning in the enumeration of its principles." As the word *sankhyá* also signifies "deliberation or judgment," the name was more probably intended to designate the result of the "deliberate judgment" of KAPILA on the great problem of the universe—with a special regard to emancipation from the evil that prevails in the world.

87.—The twenty-five 'principles' *(tattwa)* of the system, it will be observed, are comprised in the first three aphorisms (No. 6.)—viz., the 'eight producers,' the 'sixteen productions,' and 'Soul.' These twenty-five principles, according to the Sánkhya, constitute "all that is;" and KAPILA, we have seen, promises the enquirer that his final liberation from all distress will be the result of understanding "the real nature of all that is." A noticeable distinction between Kapila's way of speaking of things, and that of the Naiyáyikas, presents itself in their respective choice of a fundamental verb. The language of the Nyáya is moulded on the verb "to be," and that of the Sánkhya on the verb "to make." The Nyáya asks "what *is*?"—the Sánkhya asks "what *makes* it so?" The one presents us with a "compte rendu" of the Universe as it stands:—the other presents us with a cosmogony. As the one subdivides its subject-matter into the two exhaustive categories of Existence and Non-existence, the other exhibits everything (except 'Soul'—the spectator of the phantasmagoria) under the two aspects of 'producer' and 'production.'

The 'productions' are held to be not other than the 'producers' modified; and the producers—all except the first of them—are but modifications of the first—the *múla-prakriti*. By what process of thought the notion of such a first principle is arrived at, the following extract from Morell's History of Philosophy (Vol. I. p. 208), may serve to illustrate. Mr. Morell is there speaking of one of the latest German systems, that of Herbart.

88.—"The process by which the necessity of philosophy comes "to be felt is the following:—When we look round us upon the "world in which we live, our knowledge commences by a per-"ception of the various objects that present themselves on every "hand to our view. What we *immediately* perceive, however, is "not actual essence, but phenomena; and after a short time, we "discover that many of those phenomena are unreal; that they "do not portray to us the actual truth of things as they are; "and that if we followed them implicitly, we should soon be "landed in the midst of error and contradiction. For example, "what we are immediately conscious of in coming into contact "with the external world, are such appearances as green, blue, "bitter, sour, extension, resistance, &c. These phenomena, "upon reflection, we discover not to be so many real indepen-"dent existences, but properties inhering in certain substances, "which we term things. Again, when we examine further into "these *substances*, we discover that they are not real ultimate "essences, but that they consist of certain elements, by the "combination of which they are produced. What we term the "*reality*, therefore, is not *the thing as a whole*, but the elements "of which it is composed. Thus the further we analyse, the "further does the idea of *reality* recede backwards; but still it "must always be somewhere, otherwise we should be perceiving a "nonentity. The last result of the analysis is the conception "of an absolutely simple element, which lies at the basis of all "phenomena in the material world, and which we view as the "essence that assumes the different properties which come be-"fore us in sensation."

89.—This "essence that assumes the different properties which come before us in sensation,"—this, which the European analyst arrives at as "the last result of the analysis"—is what the Sánkhya expositor, proceeding synthetically, lays down as his first position. This primordial essence—among the synonymes for which, given in our text-book (No. 7), are the 'undiscrete,' the 'indestructible,' that 'in which all generated effect is comprehended,' &c., is the 'Absolute' of German speculation. The developement of this principle, according to one of Schelling's views (noticed by Mr. Morell at p. 147 vol. 2d) is "not the free and designed operation of intelligence, but rather a blind impulse working, first unconsciously in nature, and only coming to self-consciousness in mind." So, according to KAPILA, "from Nature issues Mind, and thence Self-consciousness" [see No. 54]:

—but here a striking difference between the European and the Oriental theory presents itself—for the Self-consciousness, which so many European philosophers assume as the only certain starting-point, and as the very characteristic of Soul, is declared by KAPILA to be no property of Soul, and to be regarded as such only through a delusion. In the 64th of the 'memorial verses' of I'S'WARA KRISHṆA, as translated by Mr. Colebrooke, KAPILA says :—

90.—"So, through study of principles, the conclusive, incon-"trovertible, one only knowledge is attained, that neither I AM, "nor is aught mine, nor do I exist."

91.—This statement M. Cousin not unnaturally regards as amounting to "le nihilisme absolu, dernier fruit du scepticisme" —but Professor Wilson, in accordance with the commentaries, declares that "It is merely intended as a negation of the soul's "having any active participation, any individual interest or pro-"perty, in human pains, possessions, or feelings." The Soul, according to the Sánkhya, might be described in the terms in which Fichte speaks of the Mind, "as it were, an intelligent eye, "placed in the central point of our inward consciousness, sur-"veying all that takes place there"—(Morell—Vol. 2. p. 95). In the words of KAPILA (Verse 19th), "Soul is witness, solitary, "bystander, spectator, and passive." Soul being thus inert, all that is done arises from the energy of the 'radical principle'—of which one might correctly speak in the terms employed by Schelling in speaking of the 'Absolute,' where he says—"The "primary form of the Absolute is *will*, or *self-action*. It is an "absolute power of becoming in reality what it is in the germ." (Morell—Vol. 2. p. 150).

92.—The 'Absolute,' the germ, in the hands of KAPILA, having reached the form of 'Self-consciousness'—*ahankára*—the 'making of an *I*,'—the 'positing of an *Ego*'—the course of subsequent developement runs parallel, for some distance, with that followed by Fichte, who takes the 'Ego' as his starting point. According to a writer in Brande's Dictionary—"To use the "language of Fichte—the ego is absolute, and posits itself: it is "a pure activity. As its activity, however, has certain indefin-"able limits, when it experiences this limitation of its activity, "it also posits a non-ego, and so originates the objective world. "The ego, therefore, cannot posit itself without at the same "time projecting a non-ego; which, consequently, is in so far "the mere creation of the ego." In like manner the *ahankára* of KAPILA creates [No. 54] out of itself the five 'subtile elements,' the bases of the gross elements,—so that the world of sense, formed out of these, is, in this as in Fichte's system, "the mere creation of the ego." A marked difference between the two systems, as observed before, consists in this—that KAPILA makes the creative 'Ego' to be something else than 'Soul,' which latter, he holds, by confounding itself with the active principle, gets entangled in the distresses of life.

93.—The motive of the Bráhman's enquiry at KAPILA, it will be remembered, is this—that he wishes he may not be "again "obnoxious to the three sorts of pain:"—in other words that he may not be born again—that he may be no more liable to transmigration or the Metempsychosis. Of the Metempsychosis Prof. Wilson (*Sánkhya Káriká* p. x.) says:—"This belief is not "to be looked upon as a mere popular superstition; it is the main "principle of all Hindú metaphysics; it is the foundation of all "Hindú philosophy." The doctrine of the Metempsychosis may be regarded as the Hindú theory on the great question of the "origin of evil." The theory may be thus stated. Evil exists—and it is not to be supposed that evil befals any one undeservedly. When, therefore, for example, a newborn child, who has had no opportunity of acting either rightly or wrongly, is found suffering evil, it is inferred that the evil is the fruit of evil deeds done in a former state of existence. If it be asked how the person became disposed to do evil in that former state of existence, the answer offered is this—it was the consequence of evil deeds done in a state of existence still anterior—and so on. Applying now the principle of 'limits'—that what is true at every assignable point short of the limit, must be true at the limit—as there is no assignable point in the existence of evil in past time for its existence at which point this hypothesis does not serve equally well to account, it is argued that, on this hypothesis, and on no other, is the existence of evil fully accounted for. To the European this method of accounting for the origin of evil appears to be vitiated by the 'regressus in infinitum' *(anavasthá)*—the same consideration which vitiates the theory of the earth's resting on the elephant, the elephant's resting on the tortoise, and so on without end. The origin of evil he regards as not having been revealed; and the requirement that we shall maintain our reliance on the goodness of God in the absence of such revelation, he regards as a trial of our faith.

94.—Several of the terms in the treatise of which a translation has been given, do not occur in the Sánkhya treatises generally studied. On these and some other points a few annotations here follow.

95.—Among the epithets applied to 'Self-consciousness' (in No. 18) are *sánumána* and *niranumána*. We can get no account anywhere of this application of these terms. Self-consciousness 'not associated with inference' might possibly refer to the simple consciousness of existence; whilst the consciousness 'associated with inference' might refer to the notion of the Egoist who has reasoned himself into the belief that he himself constitutes all that is—(see No. 17) :—but then the difficulty would remain of tracing the connexion between this sense and the functions assigned to these aspects of self-consciousness under No. 61.—The technical or 'slang' terms in Nos. 64 &c., differ in our text-book from those given in the comment on the *Kárikás*—see p. 155 of the *Sánkhya Káriká*, where Prof. Wilson says "No explanation of the words is anywhere given, nor is any reason assigned for their adoption."

96.—On the 'triad of qualities' (No. 49), Prof. Wilson, at p. 52 of the *Sánkhya Káriká*, remarks :—"In speaking of qualities, "however, the term *guṇa* is not to be regarded as an insubstantial "or accidental attribute, but as a substance discernible by soul "through the medium of the faculties. It is, in fact, nature, or "*prakriti*, in one of its three constituent parts or conditions, "unduly prominent; nature entire, or unmodified, being nothing "more than the three qualities in equipoise, according to the "Sútra, '*Prakriti* is the equal state of goodness, foulness, and "darkness.'"

97.—The term *abhibuddhi* would seen to be obsolete in the sense assigned to it in No. 58. In the copy of the work employed in making the translation, the same term *(abhibuddhi)* is repeated as representing the first of its own five subdivisions. This, with other obvious clerical errors, has been amended with the concurrence of learned pandits. The term *karttavyatá*, in the same passage, is akin to our term 'susceptibility.'

98.—'Inference' is briefly noticed in paragraph No. 77. As the writers on the Sánkhya do not appear to be all exactly of the same mind on the subject of inference, it may be worth while to examine the matter :—and, as the terms which they make use of are the same as those which are employed, with less diversity of sentiment, by the Naiyáyikas, it may be as well to begin by determining the sense in which the Naiyáyikas understand the terms.

99.—After describing 'perception,' in his fourth aphorism, Gautama, the founder of the Nyáya school, proceeds, in his fifth aphorism, to speak of 'inference' as follows :—

अथ तत्पूर्वकं त्रिविधमनुमानं पूर्ववच्छेषवत्सामान्यतो दृष्टञ्च ॥ ५ ॥

"Now 'inference,' preceded thereby [i. e., preceded by 'perception'] is of three kinds—(1) that which has the 'prior'—(2) that which has the 'posterior'—and (3) that which is [or consists in] the perception of 'community.'"

100.—'Inference,' as stated in paragraph No. 77 of our text-book, is "knowledge arising from the perception of a '*sign*;'" and as the 'sign' *(linga)*—the Greek σημειον or rather τεκμηριον —the "*mark* from which a conclusion may be drawn"—may be of three kinds; so the modes of 'inference,' as stated in the aphorism of Gautama, are likewise three.

101.—The first kind of 'sign' Gautama calls 'prior' *(púrvva)*. The meaning of the term is explained by his commentator (in the *Nyáya-sútra-vritti)* as follows :—

पूर्वं कारणं । तद्वत् तल्लिङ्गकं । यथा मेघोन्नतिविशेषेण वृष्ट्यनुमानं ।

"[By the expression in the aphorism] 'prior' [is meant] *cause* —[a cause being prior to, or the antecedent of, its effect—and, when perceived, serving as a 'sign' of the effect yet unperceived]. [By the expression in the aphorism] 'which has that' [i. e., which has the 'prior,' or cause—is meant] which has that as a 'sign'.

As (for example) the inference of rain from the circumstance of the gathering of clouds."

In this example of inference, the 'prior' (*púrvva*)—the antecedent or cause—is the 'sign;'—the gathering of clouds, the antecedent or cause of rain, being that 'sign' from which a fall of rain is inferred by anticipation. By European writers, this kind of inference is named, in terms strictly corresponding to those of the Nyáya, inference 'a priori' [i. e. the inference of the consequent *from the antecedent*].

102.—The second kind of 'sign' Gautama calls 'posterior' (*s'esha*). The meaning of the term is explained by his commentator as follows:—

शेषः कार्य्यं। तल्लिङ्गकं शेषवत्। यथा नदीवृद्ध्या वृष्ट्यनुमानं।

"[By the expression in the aphorism] 'posterior' [is meant] *effect* [—an effect being posterior to, or the consequent of, its cause—and, when perceived, serving as a 'sign' of the cause which was unperceived]. [By the expression in the aphorism] 'which has the posterior' [is meant—inference] which has that ['posterior' or consequent] as a 'sign.' As [for example] the inference of rain from the swelling of a river".

In this example of inference, the 'posterior' (*s'esha*)—the consequent or effect—is the 'sign';—the swelling of a river—the consequent or effect of rain—being the 'sign' from which a fall of rain is inferred to have gone before. By European writers, this kind of inference is named, in terms strictly corresponding to those of the Nyáya, the inference 'a posteriori' [i. e., the inference of the antecedent *from the consequent*].

103.—The third kind of 'sign' Gautama calles 'the perception of community' (*sámányato drishṭa*). The import of the term is explained by his commentator as follows:—

सामान्यतो दृष्टं कार्य्यकारणभिन्नलिङ्गकं । यथा पृथिवीत्वेन द्रव्यत्वानुमानं ।

"[By inference from] 'the perception of community' [is meant inference] where the 'sign' is other than effect or cause. As [for example] the inferring that something is a substance from its having the nature of earth".

In this example the *sámánya* or 'generic character' termed *prithivítwa* 'earthiness' is a 'sign' from which, when perceived, 'substantiality'—neither the cause nor the effect, but, in this instance, the higher genus—is inferred. The definition applies also to 'inference from analogy', as the term *sámányato drishṭa* has been rendered.

104.—The commentator from whom we have quoted mentions another opinion in regard to the names of the three kinds of inference;—that they refer to those three kinds of 'signs' (specified in page 38 of the 'Lectures on the Nyáya Philosophy'—) viz., the 'sign' which is in every case present; that which is absent in every case but one; and that which is present in some cases and absent in others. This notion—apparently originating in nothing much deeper than the consideration that there are "three to three"—may be dismissed as barely on a level with Captain Fluellen's parallel between Harry of Monmouth and Alexander of Macedon, (in 'King Henry V'—Act iv—sc. 7.), based on the consideration that "There is a river in Macedon; and there is also moreover a river at Monmouth".

105.—Of the three examples given in our text-book (No. 77) the first—viz: the inferring of 'rain from the assembling of clouds,' falls under the first division (—see No. 101.). The second example—the inferring that 'there is water because there are cranes &c.', exemplifies the second division—(see No. 102)—the presence of the cranes and such-like waterfowl being consequent on the presence of the water which these birds frequent. The third example—the inferring of 'fire from smoke'—(which the author of the *Sánkhya Pravachana Bháshya* refers to the first class)—falls under the same head as the second—smoke being met with only where there has been fire as an antecedent. The selection of examples here therefore is unsatisfactory—being at once redundant and defective.

106.—In the 5th and 6th of the 'Memorial Verses', inference is spoken of as follows:—

———————त्रिविधमनुमानमाख्यातं

तल्लिङ्गलिङ्गिपूर्व्वकं———————

सामान्यतस्तु दृष्टादतीन्द्रियाणां प्रतीतिरनुमानात् ।

Thus rendered by Mr. Colebrooke—

"Inference, which is of three sorts, premises an argument, and (deduces) that which is argued by it." * * * * "it is by inference (or reasoning) that acquaintance with things transcending the senses is obtained:"—

[Professor Wilson prefers rendering the latter clause thus:—"It is by reasoning from analogy that belief in things beyond the senses is attained."]

107.—The remarks of the scholiast GAUḌAPÁDA (in the *Sánkhya Bháshya)* on the foregoing text are as follows:—

त्रिविधमनुमानमाख्यातं शेषवत् पूर्व्ववत् सामान्यतो दृष्टं चेति । पूर्व्वमस्यास्तीति पूर्व्ववद् यथा मेघोन्नत्या वृष्टिं साधयति पूर्व्ववृष्टित्वात् । शेषवद्यथा समुद्रादेकं जलपलं लवणमासाद्य शेषस्याप्यस्ति लवणभाव इति । सामान्यतो दृष्टं । देशान्तराद्

देशान्तरं प्राप्तं दृष्टं गतिमच्चन्द्रतारकं चैत्रवत् । यथा चैत्रनामानं देशान्तराद् देशान्तरं प्राप्तमवलोक्य गतिमानयमिति तद्वच्चन्द्रतारकमिति तथा पुष्पिताम्रदर्शनादन्यत्र पुष्पिताम्रा इति सामान्यतो दृष्टेन साधयति । एतत्सामान्यदृष्टं ॥ किञ्च तल्लिङ्गलिङ्गिपूर्व्वकमिति । तदनुमानं । लिङ्गपूर्वकं यत्र लिङ्गेन लिङ्गी अनुमीयते यथा दण्डेन यतिः । लिङ्गिपूर्व्वकञ्च यत्र लिङ्गिना लिङ्गमनुमीयते यथा दृष्ट्वा यतिमस्येदं त्रिदण्डमिति ॥

"Inference, which is of three kinds, takes the name of 'that which has the consequent' (see No. 99), 'that which has the antecedent,' and 'that which is [or consists in] the perception of Community.' 'That which has the antecedent,' is that [form of inference] where [it is argued]—'That [which we are adducing as the sign] is the antecedent of this [which we wish to establish]:'—as, for example, when one proves [an approaching fall of] rain by the rising of clouds—because this [rising of clouds] is an antecedent of rain. [As an example of inference] 'which has the consequent'—[suppose that] having found a drop of water taken from the sea to be salt, the saltness of *the rest* also is inferred. 'Analogous'—as, having observed their change of place, it is concluded that the moon and stars are locomotive like CHAITRA: that is, having seen a person named CHAITRA transfer his position from one place to another, and thence having known that he was locomotive, it is inferred that the moon and stars also are locomotive. So too, observing a mango tree in blossom, one establishes the fact that other mango trees also are in flower [not by adducing, in proof of the fact either, the *cause* of the fact or any *consequence* of the fact—but] by remarking the common nature [of the mango tree under inspection—in virtue of which common nature the other mango trees blossom simultaneously with it.] Such is [inference by means of] 'the perception of Community.'

Again [the words] *tallinggapúrvvakam* &c., [may be rendered otherwise :—thus] *tad* 'that'—viz., 'inference'—*linggapúrvvaka* 'where, from a characteristic, that which possesses the characteristic is inferred,' as, [one is inferred to be] a mendicant from his staff [when his staff is of the characteristic description carried by mendicants]. And [the act of inference may be said to be] *linggipúrvvaka*, 'where, from what possesses a characteristic, the characteristic itself is inferred,' as, having seen a mendicant, you say, this [which he holds in his hand, and which, from distance or some other reason, is not clearly discernible in his grasp] is his triple staff—[for where the mendicant presents himself, there his characteristic staff is sure to be found also]."

Now, in his example of inferring the saltness of the ocean from the saltness of a drop taken from it, GAUḌAPÁDA appears to have been misled by the ambiguity of the word *s'esha,* which the Naiyáyikas employ as the opposite of *púrvva*—the opposition intended being that of antecedent, and consequent not that of part and remainder. GAUḌAPÁDA, taking the word in its familiar sense of '*the rest,*' imagines that when we infer the *rest* of the ocean to be salt like a drop taken from it, the process falls under the second head in the division of the modes of inference, whereas it falls under the third head—the same which he exemplifies by the case of the mango-trees. As we infer that other mango-trees blossom when one mango-tree blossoms, because all mango-trees have one common nature; so likewise do we infer that the other drops of the ocean are salt, when we find that one drop is salt, because all the drops in the ocean have one common nature. Thus, whilst our anonymous commentator on KAPILA gives two examples of the second kind and no example of the third, GAUḌAPÁDA gives two examples of the third kind and none of the second. For the illustration of KAPILA, therefore, some of his commentators would appear, by these discrepancies, to have borrowed the terminology of the Nyáya without considering themselves bound to adhere to the sense assigned to the terms by the inventors. Whether the writers on the Sánkhya, as has been suggested, intended, by their peculiar application of the terms of the Nyáya, to inculcate their own tenet of the indifference of cause and effect, is a point the consideration of which we remit to another occasion.